RUPTURES IN THE AMERICAN PSYCHE

RUPTURES IN THE AMERICAN PSYCHE

Containing Destructive Populism in Perilous Times

Michael J. Diamond

PHOENIX
PUBLISHING HOUSE
firing the mind

First published in 2022 by
Phoenix Publishing House Ltd
62 Bucknell Road
Bicester
Oxfordshire OX26 2DS

British Library Cataloguing in Publication Data

A C.I.P. for this book is available from the British Library

ISBN-13: 978-1-800131-27-9

Typeset by Medlar Publishing Solutions Pvt Ltd, India

www.firingthemind.com

For Linda, for Maya and Mitchell and Baby Emilia, for Alex and Kate, and for all who cherish justice, the preciousness of democracy, and our treasured planet

In a dark time, the eye begins to see,
I meet my shadow in the deepening shade.
—Theodore Roethke (1960, p. 231)

Contents

Acknowledgments

So many individuals have played an important role in stimulating my thinking, helping me contain my feelings, and encouraging my reaching out by sharing my thoughts both through teaching and in writing this book. In particular, I want to express my deepest gratitude to Pam Dirham, R. James Perkins, David Rapkin, and Jerry Shapiro, with whom I dialogued often and most usefully about key issues raised in this book. Likewise, Robert Moradi, Dan Minton, and the late Loren Woodson freely shared their thinking about these topics in ways that furthered my own understandings. In addition, the political insights of friends such as Stephen Lowe and Marilyn Levin are much appreciated, as are the wisdom and courageous commitment to truth-seeking and truth-telling of journalists and public intellectuals too numerous to name. The late Hedda Bolgar—having fled Europe in the face of Nazism and, though dying (at age 101) several years before I began this project—profoundly influenced my thinking about the essential relationship between psychoanalysis and the political environment. I also want to make explicit that my editorial assistant, Gina Atkinson, is the unsung hero of this project; her steadfast encouragement, editorial brilliance, patience, and humanity helped me stay on course.

Above all, this book could not have been written without the companionship, understanding, support, and interest in my ideas that my wife, Linda, consistently and good-naturedly provided as she lovingly endured the innumerable hours of my being lost in a haze of studying, thinking, and writing. Just as there's no baby without a mother (and father), there's no writer without a village!

About the author

Michael J. Diamond, PhD, FIPA, is a training and supervising analyst at the Los Angeles Institute and Society for Psychoanalytic Studies. He is a fellow of the International Psychoanalytical Association, the American Psychological Association, and the American Academy of Clinical Psychology. He has published more than 100 journal articles and book chapters as well as four books across wide-ranging topics, including psychoanalytic technique and analytic mindedness; trauma and dissociation; masculinity, femininity, and gender theory; fathering and the paternal function; hypnosis and altered states; and group processes and social action. He is well known for national and international presentations and is the honored recipient of numerous awards for his teaching, writing, and clinical contributions. His four previous books are: *Masculinity and Its Discontents: The Male Psyche and the Inherent Tensions of Maturing Manhood* (Routledge, 2021), *The Second Century of Psychoanalysis: Evolving Perspectives on Therapeutic Action* (Karnac, 2011), *My Father Before Me: How Fathers and Sons Influence Each Other Throughout Their Lives* (W. W. Norton, 2007), and *Becoming a Father: Contemporary Social, Developmental, and Clinical Perspectives* (Springer, 1995).

Several of his publications have been translated into other languages, including German, Portuguese, Korean, Arabic, Mandarin, and French. He has a full-time clinical practice in Los Angeles, California, where he is also active in teaching, supervising, and writing.

Preface

Writing is often a means of reducing the anxiety one experiences in grappling with an especially troubling problem. The process itself frequently helps me as a psychoanalyst to acquire a deeper, more complex rendering of the phenomenon and especially of the subjectivities—including my own—that I seek to better understand. This book represents the culmination of more than six years of study, augmented by a lifetime of personal experience. Still, much like both the psychoanalytic journey into (and with) an individual psyche and the American experiment itself, the book is far from a finished product. This is how it is with each patient and his or her psychic development. An individual psyche or a group psyche always remains *in process*, and its stability, coherence, and progress are forever precarious.

My interest in delving deeper into the polity of the United States and the populist movement that led to Donald Trump's rise to power is aptly illustrated by fragments from three clinically relevant instances that personally impacted me following Trump's effort to secure the Republican nomination for president. The reader may find familiar elements in these brief vignettes.

Vignette 1: A child reacts

A child psychoanalyst met with the parents of a six-year-old boy who had been sent home from school after "beating up" another child. The couple's son was a cute and chubby, blond-haired boy who had never before been in trouble or been particularly aggressive. However, the boy had become enraged with another boy, whom he then punched in the face twice, after the other boy said to him, "You look like Trump!"

Vignette 2: A patient with a secret

Leo, a highly successful professional in his late fifties, had met with me once weekly for nearly four years. Though he had a long and seemingly happy marriage, was a devoted father to his teenage children and a highly respected member of his religious Jewish community, he had long suffered from a deep sense of shame as an immigrant who had fled from an oppressive, authoritarian regime. Despite his accomplishments, he experienced himself as an outsider, most poignantly within his own family. With considerable guilt, he carried on a "secret life" (involving both financial assets and clandestine extramarital affairs) that he was able to share with me.

However, it wasn't until well into our third year of work (more than two years after Trump was elected) that Leo sheepishly told me something he hadn't "dared to disclose, especially to my wife and children"—or to his best friend or anyone else in his inner circle. I was taken by surprise when this socially liberal, highly educated, and thoughtful man revealed that he had "voted for Trump, donated substantially to his campaign, and unequivocally supported him" (despite Trump's defense of white-nationalist, anti-Semitic protesters at the 2017 Charlottesville rally). Leo was terrified that if his wife or children were to learn of this, they would "never forgive me—and maybe even never love me again." Not surprisingly, he was also very fearful that my understanding of him and of his dynamics and character would vanish.

Vignette 3: A dream of my own

A close friend, a Jungian analyst, recently reminded me of a dream I had shared with him a few months after Trump took office in 2017.

Interestingly, I had totally forgotten the dream. In the dream, I was seated in my home office excitedly waiting for a new patient to arrive. When the patient entered, I was somewhat shocked to see that it was Trump himself, particularly since I didn't think he'd be inclined to enter into analysis. But he did—sort of! In fact, it seemed that he was baiting me, daring me to figure out what was going on with him, but each of my attempts at understanding was met with stronger opposition as he boasted that he knew so much more than I did, and that I was wasting his time and money. I felt useless and bullied, as well as increasingly helpless.

The dream took on a nightmarish quality, and I woke up startled and befuddled as to its meaning. Only now, several years later, does it seem that the dream may have had something to do with this book—a future project I hadn't at all been conscious of at the time. In one sense, at least in part, this book reflects my own "psychoanalysis" of America's relationship to Trump and Trumpism. Most interestingly, as I will briefly discuss in my final chapter, I had a second, more benign dream four and a half years after the first one, in which Trump once again appeared in my office.

* * *

Despite Trump's central role in each of these vignettes, this book is not about him or his character, even though many psychoanalysts and other mental health clinicians could have a field day (and many have, clearly and skillfully) in speculating about, inferring from, and diagnosing this exceedingly flawed yet astonishingly skillful, persuasive human being. Who Trump is and how he persuades others to follow his lead continues to play a truly momentous role in what is happening in the US and, to some extent, worldwide. As this book will make clear, a perfect storm has made for a most dangerous fit, resulting in the populist cult of Trumpism.

Before inviting readers to join in the quest to understand and help contain what I believe to be a democratic society in peril, I wish to share a couple of personal notes. I've been writing this book as we live through an unprecedented time of global pandemic caused by the COVID-19 virus, resulting in political, economic, health care, and environmental instability. In addition, the climate crisis is mounting and wildfires flourish along the Pacific Coast of North America and elsewhere in the world; at the same time, societal inequities and social injustices render this a time of unprecedented national and international turbulence.

Though helpful in providing a modicum of solace through greater understanding and potentially hopeful activism, the process of researching, thinking, and writing this book has not provided me with a respite from my deep concerns. Still, seeing what's in plain sight, this arduous labor of love is being carried out for all those who cherish justice, the preciousness of democracy, and the treasure of our planet—and perhaps especially for those who will be born years after we who are alive today have passed on.

Throughout this endeavor, my many conversations with trusted friends and respected colleagues that involve shared understandings, divergences, and convergences in thinking and feeling—as well as anxious concerns—have proven invaluable. Here, then, as I stand on the shoulders of this groundswell of interactive support, I offer this book as provocative food for thought and, hopefully, impetus for action among those interested in learning more about what lies behind the power and influence of America's "Very Stable Genius."

Michael J. Diamond
Los Angeles, CA, USA
Fall 2021

CHAPTER 1

Introduction: exploring the non-rational, unconscious dimensions in American politics[1]

> *Individuals are unconsciously provoked to express ideas of behavior on behalf of the group dynamic.*
>
> —Philip Stokoe (2019, p. 2)

This book explores the relationship between large-group regression, cultism, destructive populism, delusional thinking, conspiratorial beliefs, authoritarianism, and leadership characterized by malignant narcissism and paranoia. I will examine the fact that Donald Trump received over 74 million votes for United States president in the 2020 election, and that *Trumpism* will continue to play a major role in the American sociopolitical landscape, even though he has exited the presidential stage.

Because a more rational understanding of former President Trump's appeal in the context of his severely compromised character causes

[1] In deference to the Unites States' southern neighbors, I'd like to mention that throughout this book, I use the words *American* and *America* as, respectively, an adjective pertaining to United States and a noun referring to *the* United States—even though these words more accurately pertain, of course, to Central and South America as well, and indeed to all the countries and regions of the Americas.

many informed and fact-oriented Americans to shake their heads in bewildered astonishment, I propose that what has happened in the US can be most accurately grasped through a *psychoanalytic way of understanding* the most primitive, largely unconscious dimensions that operate throughout larger groups and have been present in the country since its inception. Psychoanalysts, along with such eminent historians as Richard Hofstadter (1965), believe that politics tends to be an arena for the projection of impulses, feelings, and wishes that are only "marginally related to the manifest issues" (p. xxxiii).

A psychoanalytic view of recent American sociopolitics

In my view, it is essential to maintain a psychoanalytic perspective on what the United States is going through politically and socially, both for deeper insight and for successful containment of the strong reactions such matters are likely to trigger. As psychoanalyst Leon Hoffman (2018) notes, "Too often, social and political theorists have overvalued the power of the intellect to address complex social conflicts and upheavals, such as current political conflicts" (p. 267).

I will begin by addressing the overall lack of collaborative understanding between what psychoanalytic depth psychology teaches us and what we hear from many of today's leading historians and political scientists. My thinking aims to address and synthesize seminal understandings offered by psychoanalytic depth psychology with the rich interdisciplinary perspectives brought by expert historians and political scientists, as well as by social psychologists, sociologists, astute journalists, and other public intellectuals. I draw on all these sources in addressing destructive populism, malignant normality, and cultism reflective of psychotic group regression. In focusing on such deteriorations in larger groups, I will address the central pathological manifestations that we see today, including such essential psychoanalytic concepts as defensive identification, projective identification, narcissism, splitting, denial, negative hallucination, omnipotent coercion, and perverted containment, as well as what is apparent to most observers as indications of extreme mendacity, thought control, social violence, conspiratorial thinking, and corruption.

In addition to my own thinking in venturing into this more chancy terrain, I also bring to bear psychoanalytic ideas pertaining to group dynamics and leadership offered by Wilfred Bion, Sigmund Freud, Erich Fromm, Christopher Bollas, Otto Kernberg, Robert Lifton, Leo Rangell, Herbert Rosenfeld, and Vamık Volkan, as well as by José Bleger, Elliott Jaques, and several more recent Kleinian/Bionian-influenced analysts. My goal is to find ways to make use of these understandings that might help reestablish a sufficiently containing frame—steadying the nation's bough, we might say—and strengthen the body politic's nonpathological elements in order to come to grips with these very disturbing social, political, and psychodynamic factors.

This book, then, is a response to what I deem crucial for the United States (and of value worldwide)—namely, to synthesize psychoanalytic understandings with the rich thinking about political groupings from outside psychoanalysis in order to address what promises to continue to be the key question for years to come—that is, *how can we negotiate reality with the extremism of the alt-right movement rather than continuing to be faced with an irreconcilable schism?*

To shed light on what has happened and continues to foment in the nation's polity, I will explore the conditions leading to large-group regression, the long-standing nature of American populism and its relationship to authoritarianism, the unique fit between malignant leadership and perverted containment within regressed groups, the conspiratorial and psychotic processes maintaining regressed large groups, the psychic mechanisms that turn a regressed large group into a personality cult, and the unique contributions that psychoanalysis can make in managing such regressive, malevolent dynamics.

My personal journey toward an exploration of the American collective unconscious

Just prior to the 2016 election, I attended a psychoanalytic workshop in which a form of group thinking rendered most of the attendees certain that the United States would never elect someone like Trump to the presidency. I believed that the understanding presented of a very complex reality was too limited, and I was quite troubled by the overconfident certitude of the workshop's main presenter, particularly in his offer of a far too reductive thesis uncritically applying psychoanalytic concepts to Trump supporters. An obscuring focus on the *individual* psychodynamics of politicians and voters produced by multiculturalism and the dangers of "otherness" stood out, while Trump's popularity was attributed largely to the need for a father figure in the context of threatening economic factors and an insidious misogyny, xenophobia, and racism among his misguided followers that seemingly could never be "sufficient for him to triumph over Hillary Clinton."

There seemed to be an absence of sound and complex analytic thinking about large-group regression, as well as a failure to consider unconscious conflictual factors, especially in the collective polity in which democracy's linchpin resides in its dialectical nature and the essential role played by intermediary institutions. Perhaps because there was a dearth of interdisciplinary thinking brought to bear, it seemed that psychoanalytic explanations were problematically employed as an all-around psychology to account for virtually anything that might explicate Trump's popularity with his likely voters. I found myself dismayed by the degree to which a *basic assumption* mentality of "us versus them" had taken hold among a large group of otherwise highly intelligent, extremely well-educated, liberal-thinking psychoanalytic clinicians, a mentality that was also manifest among many liberal thinkers throughout the country, where the main focus seemed to be on the easily deceived, proto-authoritarian common people.[2] Still, I was cautiously hopeful in the lead-up to the election and terribly disheartened (albeit not surprised) by the results.

As the situation escalated over the next four years, I found myself struggling to better understand how what was taking place could happen here in this country. How did Trump's 2016 election materialize, and why did more than 74 million vote to elect him again in 2020 despite what was known about him? Moreover, why have so many Americans continued to support an effort to overthrow the election's results and attempt

---

[2] As I will discuss further in Chapter 2 when addressing the rise of right-wing authoritarian populism, it is disingenuous and misleading to place fundamental blame on the people themselves. Perhaps this is especially true for liberals and anti-Trumpists who tend to "revive clichés from nineteenth-century mass psychology" (Müller, 2021, p. ix). Instead, both the empowering and the constraining responsibilities for authoritarian leaders and movements lie with the checks and balances of "intermediary institutions" (ibid.), including the judiciary, the professional media, the US Congress, and political parties themselves.

to suppress subsequent voting in order to maintain Trump's power and influence? Consequently, in part to manage my own existential anxieties in following the news and observing pathologically regressive processes occurring throughout the nation, I continue what I began more than six years ago in studying the works of profound political thinkers across the spectrum of social science and politics, while returning to some of my roots in interdisciplinary studies as I delve deeper into seminal psychoanalytic insights about social and political groups and their functioning.

My interest in and appreciation for interdisciplinary ways of studying collective issues, and especially the nation's psyche, began nearly a half century earlier through my exposure to the Frankfurt School of critical theorists. One of these theorists, R. Nevitt Sanford, helped author a classic study, *The Authoritarian Personality* (Adorno et al., 1950). While I was pursuing my doctorate in both clinical psychology and social-personality psychology, Sanford taught a seminar shortly before founding Berkeley's Wright Institute, now a well-known graduate school in psychology.

Although I didn't realize it at the time, I was profoundly influenced by the social/clinical perspectives brought to bear on what was then at the forefront of the late 1960s political zeitgeist, and especially by the principal thinkers from the Frankfurt School. These included Theodor Adorno, Erich Fromm, Herbert Marcuse, Leo Löwenthal, Max Horkheimer, and later Jürgen Habermas, all of whom sought to articulate the inherently flawed character of civilization, and especially of large political groupings that *cannot* be reduced to individuals within the group. Though I hadn't yet become immersed in psychoanalytic understanding in which curiosity, skepticism, and humanism forcefully coexist, my inclination to question authority and challenge absolutist claims coalesced smoothly with the work of these thinkers. I saw that their research and theory might be drawn on to counteract authoritarian trends associated with totalitarianism and utopian forms of thinking, which were full-blown in the countercultural movements that I was ambivalently part of as well. Moreover, I am able to look back now and realize that I was unconsciously internalizing ways to assimilate diversified, critical forms of analytical thinking regarding absolute claims and more rational forms of traditionalism; I was thinking, in short, along lines that would portend my movement toward psychoanalysis in the decade ahead. Indeed, this unique group of critical-thinking scholars and researchers notably looked to Freud, both for clinical insights and metapsychology.[3]

Remaining socially and politically informed as well as somewhat active in these arenas, I found that my subsequent journey as a clinician, researcher, and theoretician led me toward deeper insights about underlying unconscious factors, including more malignant and pathological dimensions impacting both individual and group behavior. However, before I began exploring the unconscious factors in play, just as I was finishing my dissertation in the spring of 1970, President Nixon ordered the military to invade neutral Cambodia—a move that instigated large-scale student protests across the country. Within weeks, the Kent State Massacre had occurred and subsequent protests turned violent on college campuses, including my own, Stanford University. While participating in the protests, I was deeply troubled by how fiercely polarizing the situation had become, especially as I observed that my anti-war fellow students and activists were very similar in age and demographics to members of the property-protective campus police enforcers who faced off against them. Each group seemed to operate along more totalitarian lines reflective of mass psychology—"be on my side or be on yours," "be a peace-loving hippie or a war-mongering pig," with seemingly no common meeting ground. Autistic forms of hostility and emerging violent actions were increasing in an alarming way.

Then as now, I struggled to employ whatever I could to rectify the situation, asking myself and others how such extreme and fierce polarization might be reduced. Encouraged by Phil Zimbardo, the activist social psychologist on my dissertation committee, these efforts led to a collaborative social action project with a fellow graduate student in which we sought to bring activist, antiwar students together with the local (San Jose, CA) police force to promote understanding and greater respect (Diamond & Lobitz, 1973). Theorizing that if common ground could be found between these two separate camps of primarily young adults,

---

[3] A significant movement within contemporary psychoanalysis seeks to study the impact on the individual psyche of social structures, power relations, and ideologies, as well as the manifestations of these factors in the clinical encounter. This advance is fittingly referred to by Lynne Layton (2020) as "social psychoanalysis."

perhaps familiarity might breed respect and reduce demonization of the "other" side.

Consequently, we arranged for students and local police to gather in very small groups, both on campus and off, including the opportunity for a couple of students at a time to ride with police officers in their squad cars, often discussing what it was like to be a young person in the Bay Area. Data was collected and, as we had hoped, significant depolarization of attitudes and resultant behavior occurred under these circumstances. Communication and contact could indeed facilitate destigmatization and increase understanding—though as a young idealist, I had little appreciation for the massive force of resistance to change residing in both the individual and the group unconscious.

Over the ensuing decades, I became increasingly troubled by the authoritarian and more totalitarian social and cultural trends achieving prominence, including those within each individual and in the field of psychoanalysis itself. Not surprisingly, then, my own work across several specialty domains—including analytic technique and training, trauma and dissociation, metapsychology and psychic structure, and masculinity, gender, and fathering—would often focus on the limitations of binary thinking while also attempting to address the psyche's resistances to encompassing uncertainty, complexity, fluidity, conflict, and plurality. This naturally applies to the body politic in which the demands made upon both the individual and the collective group psyche are considerable. Consequently, psychoanalytic understandings, especially those informed by insights from group analysis, are especially apt; simultaneously, they point our profession toward a future that incorporates "a praxis of thinking that can apply to civilizations and their discontents" (González, 2020, p. 1110). Parallel to the thinking of numerous analysts who venture beyond the consulting room, my own view is that there is a strong continuity between individual psychoanalysis and psychoanalytic understandings applied to social, political, and national groups and their functioning. This book illustrates our shared belief in a variety of ways.

While the most creative political uses of psychoanalytic thinking have come from social and political theorists and activists outside the formal institutions of psychoanalysis, several mainstream analysts have made substantial contributions. For example, Leo Rangell, an esteemed colleague and teacher, in *The Mind of Watergate* (1980) examined the influence of the group on the individual mind in studying the relationship between corrupt, dishonest political leadership and irrational, neurotic dynamics, both of which are located within the analyst's "total field of observation" (p. 9). In discerning the syndrome he termed "the compromise of integrity," Rangell offered a compelling picture of societal pathology reflective of "the sick society" (p. 11). Such a group form of malignant pathology remains an especially formidable challenge unless the unique tools of psychoanalysis are brought into play in addressing it.

Applied psychoanalysis: promises and pitfalls

While caution is needed and methodological issues must be seriously considered when applying psychoanalytic principles to social and political life, a particularly useful prototype for such application is more likely when today's psychoanalysts (much like mid-twentieth-century analysts such as Erik Erikson, Erich Fromm, and several others whose thinking I will discuss later in this book) intermingle and cross-pollinate psychoanalytic knowledge with that of adjacent fields in the social sciences and humanities. In this respect, we have much to learn from the successful efforts made by the Frankfurt School and Harvard University's now defunct Department of Social Relations (as well as from their failed endeavors).

As I hope to elucidate in this book, psychoanalysis promises an alternative to authoritarian, anti-democratic processes that run rampant in contemporary American neoliberal, often more totalitarian states of mind, and especially in today's extreme right-wing, more destructive forms of populism—referred to by the Frankfurt School thinkers as the *lunatic fringe* (Löwenthal & Guterman, 1949). In an attempt to find the unconscious basis for the disturbing rise of these processes in the UK and Europe, the British Psychoanalytical Society has held a series of "Political Mind Seminars" since 2015. The success of these forums led to two valuable volumes, edited by British analyst David Morgan, that address the need for psychoanalytic thinking in social and political life (2019, 2021). Recently, here in the United States, my colleague Pam Dirham and I put this promise into action by developing a course offered locally and nationally to psychoanalysts and other mental health professionals entitled "Dancing in the Dark: Psychoanalytic Musings on Group Regression, Madness, and Chaos in the Time of COVID-19." Although we initially presented the course prior to the 2020 election, we expanded it after the election under the revised title: "It Can Happen Here—and Did: Psychoanalytic Musings on Large-Group Regression, Populist Madness, Cultism, and American Authoritarianism." Then, in the spring of 2021, the course morphed into "Psychoanalytic Musings on Trumpism, Delusions, and Malignant Populism."

Pam Dirham's valuable insights and our collaboration furthered my work along these lines and have led directly to this book. It is my hope that, by examining how the forces of group political movements are bound up with the unconscious workings of individual and group psyches, and by retaining the skeptical yet humanistic perspectives at the foundation of psychoanalysis, this book will facilitate more successful management and containment of the deep ruptures and prevailing schisms in our country's collective psyche. Without such containment that preserves essential ideals and foundational structures, the survival of our liberal democracy is in question.

The objectives of this book—and a brief overview

My aim in writing this book, then, is to further the efforts of psychoanalysts both in the United States and beyond to stay the course and together utilize our unique tools to confront, manage, and ultimately contribute to transforming the inherently destructive forces within societal groupings. However, my goal is to provide ideas that extend well beyond arguments targeting a strictly psychoanalytic audience; that is, I aim to reach social and political thinkers, as well as activists, who are deeply concerned about what have arisen as consensually validated threats to the United States as a liberal democracy. Without reducing the complexities to a tidy set of themes and motivations, my hope is to aid in the provision of conceptual tools that might lead to greater understanding and effective strategies and tactics for addressing these dangers.

My critical analysis of the large-group dynamics operative among divergent sectors of the Republican Party's right wing stems largely from my perspective as a psychoanalyst and social observer. In fact, many conservative Republican thinkers are concerned that something has gone terribly wrong in that, in a way we could not have foretold even as little as a year ago, the very core of our society is now in grave peril. Still, too few Americans who aren't serious political thinkers or philosophers have given complex and sustained thought to what democracy actually consists of and requires in order for it to be maintained (Müller, 2021).

As I will make clear in subsequent chapters, conservative ideas are essential to a liberal democracy; however, as I also attempt to elucidate, an ultraconservative and extremist segment of the Republican Party has been coopted by destructive, irrational social forces, and therefore—as painful as it is for me to articulate this—in its especially perverted form, it threatens the very foundations of democracy in the US and worldwide. The ideas I will offer are relevant if we are to seriously address these dangers arising among varying sectors that have coalesced to produce an overwhelming need for a more lasting form of containment—a containment, that is, of unleashed and powerful, largely unconscious forces operating through large-group phenomena.

In this first chapter, I have begun by noting the crucial need to view what has happened in American politics through a psychoanalytic lens, while describing the trajectory of my personal journey in this direction, ultimately culminating in the writing of this book. While then noting the dangers inherent in various forms of applied psychoanalysis, I also recognize the advantage of a cross-pollination between various aspects of the social sciences and the humanities with psychoanalysis. I include a brief statement of my objectives in writing this book.

In Chapter 2, after considering the historical connection between democracy and populism, I focus on the conditions leading to present-day populism and Trump's victory in the 2016 election, as well as his continued popularity and enduring grip on the Republican Party. In particular, I address how we might comprehend the perfect fit between Trump and the regressed group that clings to authoritarian and more paranoid forms of thinking as a way of making sense of their world. What lies behind the notable increase in conspiratorial thinking in the US today, and how does it relate to a heightened collective paranoia?

Chapter 3 offers a psychoanalytic perspective on populism in the American situation and how it can turn destructive. In considering the broader topic of group psychodynamics and the potential for regressive psychotic processes in large groups, I deepen my discussion of the presence of paranoid and conspiratorial thinking and further examine their effects. I also highlight what we have witnessed as attacks on consensual reality and democratic ideals, leading to a degradation of democracy in which its essential tensions are no longer tolerated, and malignant regression is rendered more liable to occur. How have these factors contributed to today's *American malignant normality*?

Chapter 4 more specifically examines the destructive, psychotic processes in the larger group/nation, including perversion and poorly regulated regression; I introduce the possibility of a relationship between such regression and cultism. Because a given group's members seek to deal with the activation of terrifying emotions by creating a shared defensive distortion of key aspects of reality, an acceptance of the group leader's agitating demagoguery—which offers a shameless freedom from moral constraints—becomes more likely, as does mob rule and violent insurrection. Additionally, this chapter addresses how regressive, psychotic processes operate not only among Trumpists, but among anti-Trumpists as well.

Chapter 5 explores the crucial need for containment of democracy's essential tensions when such malignant processes are involved. When there is a fit between the group's unconscious fantasies and malignant, narcissistic leadership, the stage is set for the development of cultism and a cult of personality. I focus on what is described as a *destructive populist fit* in today's post-truth era, and I discuss how a malignant leader such as Trump serves to "pervert" the containing function, which in effect produces a "rotten" *second skin*. In contrast to offering a healthy "skin," a frame, or a container that neutralizes potentially destructive, psychotic anxieties and fantasies, the malignant cult leader fuels these anxieties and fantasies to increase authoritarian rule. Trump's autocratic methodology is discussed at length, particularly in relation to its propensity to erode the features of democracy that we have long taken for granted in the US.

Chapter 6 utilizes the aforementioned ideas to inform a discussion of how we might address, encompass, and restrain America's regressive, malignant dynamics and thereby better contain Trumpism and the threat to the nation's democracy posed by destructive populism. Possible alternative approaches are presented that might reduce the potency of the toxic, psychotic elements and strengthen the healthier, nonpathological components in the collective psyche to better enable the inherent tensions of a pluralistic, liberal democracy to coexist in a competitive and cooperative manner, neither needing to crush one another nor eradicate conflict or resentment. This monumental challenge, much like that inherent in psychoanalysis itself, requires combining humanitarian impulses with insights into unconscious group dynamics, leadership, and the conflictual tensions in the American polity.

Finally, Chapter 7 offers a brief summary of this book's main ideas, along with my closing reflections on how we might make use of these understandings, both at present and in the future. I contend that a realistic, hopeful path forward demands insightful, committed action in which utopian fantasies and illusions of unity are appropriately countered, and the primitive, nonrational, and unconscious forces within our democratic, pluralistic society are dealt with in an inquiring and concerned fashion so that differences can be held in tension.

I close with an Appendix—a Glossary—which should aid readers in straddling the unique vocabularies of psychoanalysis and political science. My descriptions here are necessarily brief, intended merely to introduce the reader to key terms in both fields.

CHAPTER 2

Democracy and populism: sociopolitical perspectives on the American experiment

Given the right conditions, any society can turn against democracy.
—Anne Applebaum (2020, p. 14)

Populism as a large-group phenomenon has primarily been studied from historical, sociological, political science, philosophical, and economic perspectives. Research has shown that authoritarian, anti-democratic trends can easily emerge under certain social conditions. Such conditions can result in the rise of populistic movements as a response to varied factors in governmental rule, these movements can serve as a fertile breeding ground for demagoguery. Knowledge based largely on meritocracy (which can evolve into technocracy), coupled with the rule of the majority formed out of popular consensus and the majority's instincts, can lead to populist revolts against expertise.

In fact, distinguished historian Sophia Rosenfeld (2019) has observed that when the population at large and representative powers on high fail to be effectively contained together, partly through the lack of a commitment to verifiable truth and truth telling, there is a danger of being left with either a *neoliberal technocracy*, with its managerial elites such as economists, engineers, and corporate leaders ruling non-pluralistically in an anti-egalitarian fashion at the expense of the people, or, alternatively, *populism* will hold sway, with its anti-intellectual and anti-expertise ethos cast in an autonomous, false informational manner that often obviates constitutional rights. That something like this has occurred in the US in the twenty-first century shouldn't come as a complete surprise.

Inherent populism, democracy, and the American experiment

American democracy from its beginning was rooted in a populist epistemology. This is evident both in Thomas Paine's pamphlet on *Common Sense* (1776) and in the Founding Fathers' ever-present anti-federalist outlook in seeking to give credence to practical wisdom and intuition. In establishing the American experiment as a *representative democracy*,[1] the founders recognized the inherent tension between two sectors, each with its own form of wisdom: first, the elected, ruling political class of elites—the governmental aristocracy who ideally are virtuous, wise, and learned; and second, the ordinary common people exercising their voting rights—the populace comprised of the people (Hamilton et al., 2003).

German political philosopher Jan-Werner Müller (2021) argues that the preservation of democracy requires complex and sustained thought as to what democracy actually consists of. In his brilliant analysis, he posits that a truly democratic system requires *liberty*, *equality*, and perhaps most surprisingly, *uncertainty* (which, in contrast to chaos or randomness, is also central to the theory and practice of psychoanalysis). Uncertainty is inherent in democratic politics because, by definition, a candidate's loss of a valid election is always possible, and there are certain forms of losing in which loss must be accepted. However, democracy is "degraded," according to Müller (p. 61), when an agitating leader like Trump insists that it is not possible for him to lose an empirically

---

[1] America's democratic governance is a form of representative politics known as *republicanism* (stemming from the ideals of Kantian Enlightenment), in which the two sectors of the polity work in tandem, pursuing truth together by eradicating falsehood and error (S. Rosenfeld, 2019).

validated election; instead, in the event of such an outcome, the election can only have been "rigged" or "stolen."

Protecting the uncertainty along with the dialectic tension that lies at the very foundation of democracy, especially through broad access to voting and respect for consensual election results, further renders democracy dynamic and fluid. Müller aptly challenges the myth that sustaining democracy somehow requires defeating populism, when in fact populism is vital to ensure the fluid, messy, dynamic, and creative character that democracy demands.

Democracy is inherently a form of *institutionalized uncertainty* (Przeworski, 1991) that distinctly contrasts with autocracy, in which there is a fundamental certitude about substantive outcomes. In contrast to the dynamic and unpredictable aspects of democracy, including populism, *authoritarianism* seeks to render politics (as characterized by its individual citizens and groups) predictable. Political scientist Andreas Schedler (2013) points out that it is "the politics of uncertainty [that] transcends the boundaries between democratic and authoritarian regimes" (p. 26).

As I will subsequently elaborate, democracy inevitably involves ongoing, oscillating frictions in which its citizens use their freedoms in ways that produce inherent conflicts (especially pertaining to liberty, equality, and security) and persistent uncertainties that require structure and containment. Müller contends that democracy's "intermediary institutions"—relying on rules, norms, and standards entrusted particularly to political parties and their leaders, the professional media, and the judiciary—are crucial in upholding the needed structuring and containment functions.

In contrast to *autocratic, absolutist states*, a key characteristic of a modern *representative democracy* such as the US is "a commitment to an undogmatic, open-ended conception of truth" (S. Rosenfeld, 2019, p. 26)—one that honors the wisdom of both the people *and* the elites. Plausible facts must be relied upon, rather than bizarre untruths. (Unfortunately, Trump has often promoted the latter in what Müller [2021] satirically terms *info-feces*.) Nonetheless, there has always been ongoing tension between the rule of experts purporting truth in science, on the one hand, and other forms of elite, empirically verifiable, everyday experience of the common man, on the other (though, of course, women and black Americans have historically been left out of that equation).

Historically, the effort was to create a balance between the educated elites operating within an Enlightenment culture that favored verifiable truths, and *the real people*; consequently, each sector would contribute to determining truth (ibid.).

In short, there has always been a significant populist pole in the US political dialectic that—in contrast to the expertise of elites in government, science, academia, and the like—favored common sense, practical experience, and conceptions of truth derived from faith, intuition, and biblical revelation. When the tension between these two poles breaks down—or, in our psychoanalytic language, fails to be adequately contained—there is often a rise of populist fervor in the form of an anti-intellectual and faith-based effort to reject elitism. Moreover, as I will explicate in the next chapter, when the tensions or conflicts cannot be sufficiently tolerated by either one or both sides of the dialectic through a fundamental commitment to democracy's core tenets, extreme group regressions become more likely. As previously noted, such populist movements have characterized US history from the beginning and have included the popularity of the following, among others: Jacksonian democracy in the 1830s–1850s in which white male suffrage expanded under Andrew Jackson (president from 1829 to 1837); the nativist Know-Nothings of the 1850s; the People's Party of the 1890s; Prohibitionists in the early twentieth century; McCarthyism in the 1950s; and George Wallace's Segregationists in the 1960s (Hofstadter, 1965).

Populism and democracy: an unsteady alliance

Populism and democracy coexist in a multitude of ways in which populism takes varied forms. As I've indicated, however, most significantly it is a historical norm that is inherent to democracy in principle. Even so, it can also manifest as radically different from and mutually exclusive to democracy, in addition to its being an ambivalent phenomenon that can serve as a warning signal that changes are necessary (the "good" of populism) or a danger sign and a threat to democracy itself (the "bad" of populism). Populist methods tend to be characterized by very simple slogans, and when it takes hold over larger groups, there is a turning away from institutional expertise; in contrast, personal beliefs, faith, and emotional appeals rise to become privileged over objective facts. When the dialectical relationship between populism and democracy largely unravels, a more radical shift ensues, and what now counts as the truth that shapes public opinion is determined primarily by group loyalty and a *tribal epistemology* (S. Rosenfeld, 2019). When it lacks a commitment to verifiable truth, the otherwise generative conflict that creates both division and cohesion more likely undermines the very foundation of democracy; consequently, when the authoritarian edge of populism takes hold, the indispensable loyal opposition to the government in power instead can become an opposition to the democratic political system itself.

In order to successfully create a destructive populist movement, the out-group, against which the in-group is pitted, must be *dehumanized*. However, because dehumanizing another human being is more difficult if that individual is known, and because the process requires "(re) programming," power is more easily acquired by attaching "a stigma, a taint of pollution to an entire group" (Wilkerson, 2020, p. 141). Moreover, when a group is dehumanized, every individual within the group is debased, as is seen in pejorative terms such as *radical democrats* and *liberal elites*, and in the negative use of political labels such as *socialists* and *communists*—or, among anti-Trumpists, terms such as *deplorables*, *white supremacists*, or *white trash*. By dint of this dehumanizing process, members of the in-group become "slaves to groupthink" (p. 142) and more distanced from their own humanity as they dehumanize the *other* as a group or an individual.

How has this malignant process become so prominent in the US in the twenty-first century?

America's twenty-first-century movement to the right

Today, in the twenty-first century, populist movements are in evidence worldwide and are often accompanied by changing conceptions of truth. As I will elaborate both in this and the subsequent chapter, such processes have taken a major role in the US due to increasing multiculturalism and pluralism, more complex politics (characterized by relativism and excessive partisanship), and more pronounced income inequality (through less-regulated capitalism)—all of which add to mounting *existential anxieties* among so many in the form of *normative threats*, *dominant group status threats*, and *racialized economics*.

Among various factors, the move rightward in this country during the first two decades of the twenty-first century has set the stage for the rise of a large populist movement, which is occurring in response to the enactment of an increasing number of egalitarian policies and economic inequities. Another factor at play is changing demographics, which result in an experienced threat to the "white majority" (a majority status projected to end by 2042, or earlier in several parts of the country). This perceived threat was furthered by the election of a non-white, African American president, Barack Obama, in 2008 and his reelection in 2012. In familiar rhetoric from early in this century, the ultraconservative Tea Party vowed to "take our country back."

With Obama's victories and high approval ratings, the veneer began to slip from the undercurrent of deep-seated, enduring fears heightened by irrefutable evidence of a changing nation. For a great many, this unmasking was no longer hidden in plain sight as it seemed to have been—for example, in the racialized demonization of Obama as the "food-stamp president," the Birtherism movement, and the dog-whistle emphasis on "Barack *Hussein* Obama" (or in his characterization as "President Blackenstein" in Bill Maher's clever parody). Consequently, a virulent *backlash* was primed to occur once Obama left office—a countermovement in which long-standing authoritarian and anti-democratic trends, no longer so carefully veiled, had become ripe for exploitation.

Taking a historical view, we should be aware that political scientists, historians, and other observers of the US political landscape have documented various anti-democratic trends and accompanying strategies that gained potent footholds in the mid- to late twentieth century. This has led to the creation or extension of varied, more systematic programs associated with people such as Newt Gingrich, Karl Rove, the Koch Brothers, and the Mercer family, among others.

In addition, the Republican Party's promotion and passage of changes to election laws (along with deletion from the rolls of nearly 16 million voters between 2014 and 2016, mostly from marginalized and immigrant groups) set the stage for the 2016 election and the powerful appeal of a leader such as Donald Trump to a large swath of the US. Substantial increases in the number of hate groups opposed to multiculturalism and immigration added fuel to the fire. According to Pulitzer Prize scholar Isabel Wilkerson (2020), Trump's election reflected "a remarkable blueprint of caste hierarchy in America" (p. 330), in which voting preference was not predicted by monetary income but rather by *caste status*. This is evident when one examines these two factors among those predominantly white members of the dominant caste who voted for him.[2]

Although there are many ways to understand what I will explore in terms of large-group regression (in the form of populism and Trump's leadership), the perfect storm of a deluded, destructive populism is arguably not fueled primarily by *economic* anxieties, but rather by *existential* anxieties. It is useful to appreciate that while economics play a role in what I am describing, along with social caste (or class), actual economic deprivation is less significant than what has been termed *relative deprivation*, in which individuals feel deprived of their hopes and expectations in the context of what they perceive are benefits enjoyed by others (Pettigrew, 2017). In short, the evidence is weak that today's far-right populist, authoritarian wave is fueled by economic distress (Stenner & Haidt, 2018). Such phenomena, I believe, can best be understood through the lenses of both social science and psychoanalysis, as I will elaborate in what follows.

Authoritarianism and its role in American politics

Authoritarianism is best understood as a dynamic response in which an enduring latent yet fundamental predisposition is activated under certain, more transient environmental conditions. In the larger political context, it is typically triggered by threats and fear in which political plurality is rejected by reducing lawful rules and norms, separation of powers, and democratic voting. Authoritarianism was originally studied by the Frankfurt School associated with the Institute for Social Research

[2] Wilkerson employs the notion of caste as an organizing principle of structural racism, viewing the latter as an epiphenomenon of the structure of caste (Hoffman, 2021). In short, being white and dominant is powerfully seductive and helps to explain why individuals and groups—even non-whites and recent immigrants—will vote against their own interests in order to strengthen their status and be part of or closer to the dominant, white caste (Rao, 2021).

in Frankfurt am Main, Germany, through the lens of totalitarianism in the aftermath of Hitler's Germany. Largely influenced by critical social theory as well as by Freud's theories of ego development, authoritarianism was deemed a personality type as measured by the F-scale (for fascism) and characterized by deference to authority, aggression toward out-groups, rigidly hierarchical viewpoints, and resistance to new experience (Adorno et al., 1950; Pettigrew, 2017).

By the end of the twentieth century, the Frankfurt School—as well as critical social theory and philosophically informed social research—had begun to be disparaged, and the F-scale measure was seen as methodologically inadequate; for instance, it was regarded as limited by tautology with its dependent variables (Stenner, 2005). However, in recent years, the ongoing international crises occurring in liberal democracies—marked by increasing economic inequities and poorly regulated free-market capitalism—have led to a resurgence of interest in "cultural studies" of mass or popular culture (which, as I imply, can encourage psychoanalysts to integrate their twenty-first-century knowledge with interdisciplinary studies of critical social phenomena). In addition, as I will discuss, authoritarianism can be more usefully viewed dynamically and studied by methodologies that yield a heuristic, yet empirically based vision.

Individuals with an *Authoritarian Personality* (Adorno et al., 1950) tend to show characteristics of subordination, conventionalism, and aggression toward outsiders, supported by images of enemies and contempt toward those seen as weaker. Strict obedience to perceived authority is adhered to at the expense of personal freedom, and group authority replaces individual autonomy. Moreover, because central elements of democracy tend to be anathema to authoritarians, persons scoring high on the F-scale within a democratic society seem more susceptible to political authoritarianism under suitable regressive conditions, most likely due to narcissistically based superego constellations promoted by cultural patterns (King & Schmid Noerr, 2020, p. 751).

Social psychologists using varied scales to measure the authoritarian trait found that even before the rise of Trump, voters who identified themselves as Republicans averaged higher on authoritarianism than Democrats. More recently, Trump supporters and right-wingers throughout the world have scored higher on authoritarianism than have left-wingers (Pettigrew, 2017; Stenner & Haidt, 2018). Likewise, the related trait of *social dominance orientation* (SDO) addresses a preference for the societal hierarchy of groups and domination over lower-status groups—in short, a predisposition toward anti-egalitarianism within and between groups in the context of viewing the world in a "dog-eat-dog" manner (Pettigrew, 2017, p. 108). Social psychologists have found that Trump supporters score highly on SDO measures as well as on authoritarian scales, and right-wing voting patterns can be predicted by the joint power of these two indices (ibid.).

Contemporary theorists and researchers have offered a particularly useful and more psychoanalytically compatible way of understanding the rise of authoritarian elements in the US today. For example, Australian political psychologist and behavioral economist Karen Stenner (2005; Stenner & Haidt, 2018), in attempting to explain the country's extreme intolerance apparently arising suddenly out of nowhere, has employed a fundamental social psychology and behavioral economics model of person-situation-interaction. Using this model, Stenner posited a theory of the *authoritarian dynamic* in which an enduring, fundamental predisposition is activated under certain transient environmental conditions that are perceived as existentially threatening.

For example, in an atmosphere of societal conditions perceived as dangerous, such as rising multiculturalism, the predisposition to authoritarianism is more likely to become activated among white voters. The result is then a greater polarization between authoritarians and non-authoritarians. Research on the authoritarian predisposition among white voters suggests that both authoritarians and non-authoritarians tend to become increasingly polarized when societal conditions become more threatening (i.e., in situations of *normative threat*); however, under reassuring societal conditions, polarization attenuates and authoritarianism tends to remain latent (Stenner & Haidt, 2018).

As indicated in Chapter 1, it is misleading to explain the rise of authoritarian populism by pointing to individualized personality traits such as proto-authoritarianism. Notwithstanding this caveat, I next consider why it is useful to explore the relationship between individualized authoritarian trends and malignant forms of populism.

Authoritarianism is neither intrinsically leftist nor rightist, nor is it a set of ideas or a personality trait. Instead, Stenner regards it as an often more latent frame of mind for people who, particularly when identified with a large group experiencing existential threats to their survival, cannot tolerate complexity; consequently, obedience, conformity, and sameness become favored over freedom and difference. In seeking security and safety through the encouragement of uniformity and the disparagement of differences, authoritarians do not embody a "closed-mindedness" in order to avoid change, but rather tend to be more "simple-minded" in avoiding the complexity and unpredictability that democracy requires (Applebaum, 2020; Stenner, 2005).

What is particularly significant in examining the current American situation is a research finding that approximately 33 percent or one third, of the white populations in Western democracies—for instance, the portion of the American voting public that supports Trump regardless of his outlandish behavior—demonstrates a predilection for authoritarianism and is resistant to interpersonal differences *when perceiving* normative threat.

According to Stenner's extensive research, the authoritarian predisposition is primarily the result of cognitive inhibitions and personality factors, noticeably heritable, that significantly limit the ability to tolerate ambiguity, complexity, and diversity; consequently, they result in congruent values and voting behavior. When perceiving sensed or assumed loss of identity, of social cohesion, and of confidence in leadership and institutions that have begun to challenge one's "way of life" (i.e., existential—or normative—threats), 33 percent of samples from Europe and the US, studied in 2005 and 2016, represented people who tended to become highly intolerant of racial, political, and moral differences (Stenner, 2005; Stenner & Haidt, 2018; see also Applebaum, 2020).

For instance, according to measures used in sampling white respondents across twenty-nine liberal democracies in 2016, "about a third … proved to be authoritarian to some degree … in their value choices" (Stenner & Haidt, 2018, p. 192). This was further confirmed in 2016–2017 in examining the probability of voting for populist candidates and causes in the US, England, and France—that is, voting for Trump, Brexit, or Le Pen, respectively (ibid.).

The impact of authoritarianism in the 2016 American election was greatly magnified under conditions of perceived normative or existential threat; thus, about 87 percent of those disillusioned respondents distrustful of their government and of the country's direction who were likely to vote for Trump were authoritarians, while only about 7 percent of them could be seen as non-authoritarians. As I've noted, Stenner argues that the perception of normative threat, often exacerbated by demagoguery, increases polarization (which exacerbates such a threat), while conversely, the impact of authoritarianism is flattened and polarization is lessened under more reassuring societal conditions, at least among white voters.

We can observe, then, that the authoritarian frame of mind, especially in its group countenance, is activated through normative threats in which terrifying fears are exacerbated through perceived failures in societal consensus, leadership confidence, and institutional trust. As noted, in this context there is a limited ability to tolerate ambiguity, complexity, and sociocultural diversity. Because liberal democracies, especially those characterized by multiculturalism, require tolerance for conflicting points of view and contradictory forces pulling in opposing directions, considerable challenges are presented to those steeped in or prone to authoritarianism under certain conditions. Moreover, a certain portion of residents in democratic countries, perhaps roughly a third, are always likely to find diversity difficult to tolerate. Consequently, anti-democratic tendencies become more salient, and when they are activated by perceived threat, may be accompanied for many by a willingness to support extremely illiberal measures, such as the obstruction of voting rights in Georgia, Texas, and Arizona, as well as excessive and violent actions, such as the January 6, 2021 attack on the US Capitol.

For individuals preferring unity and a society held together by a single, perhaps utopian vision with an ultimate solution to ubiquitous problems, modern discourse itself, with its revival of nostalgia, disappointment with meritocracy, increasing multiculturalism, and the appeal of conspiratorial thinking—along with intense public dissent and the clashing, complex cacophony of voices—renders the twenty-first-century US particularly ripe for the inflammation of authoritarian impulses and movements (Applebaum, 2020; Rhodes, 2021; see also Stenner & Haidt, 2018). In line with the complications of facing up to the reality principle, Pulitzer Prize-winning historian and journalist Anne Applebaum (2020) describes modern politics as a "jangling, dissonant sound" (p. 117)—one particularly difficult to bear for those most challenged by complexity and conflictual tensions.

Authoritarian, illiberal politicians worldwide are winning over numerous followers (many of whom might be thought of as "closet authoritarians") by bringing to bear conspiratorial theories, political polarization, and nostalgia to strengthen the wish of individuals to change their societies. Often, members of the intellectual and educated elite are recruited to help launch warfare against the rest of the educated and intellectual elite. These illiberal enablers of the "New Right" in Western democracies, including Poland, Hungary, the United Kingdom, and the US, operate inside governments, ruling coalitions, and mainstream political parties, relying on the "Big Lie" or even more "medium-sized lies" to encourage undermining or overthrowing existing institutions, laws, standards, and norms (ibid.).

The paranoid style and conspiratorial thinking in American populist movements

A particular form of authoritarianism characterized by its totalitarian and anti-democratic components is founded on delusional, conspiratorial, and paranoid forms of thinking that can be exploited by a populist leader. This has been evident throughout American history, but today's large-group regression in the form of a populist movement often characterized by a mob mentality can be best understood by combining sophisticated historical inquiry with psychoanalytic understandings of group mentality, largely through extrapolating from clinical manifestations of destructive psychopathology to the social and political realm.

This uniquely American authoritarianism—and concomitant conspiratorial as well as delusional notions—stems from both aspirational and more problematically grandiose, omnipotent ideals. These are evident in venerable slogans of "American exceptionalism," "the greatest country in the world," "America first," and "the most powerful force for good." Ironically, the unrealistically inflated nature of such slogans is evident when we examine the many ways that the quality of life in the US lags behind that of other leading countries. For instance, in addition to hosting the world's largest coronavirus outbreak, consider that the US falls behind many countries along indices such as incarceration rates, life expectancy, maternal and infant mortality rates, healthcare provision, deaths by gunshot, students' math and reading scores, and self-reports of happiness.

Populist waves giving rise to authoritarian-based, more extreme right-wing movements tend to be activated by core elements of liberal democracy itself, such as diversity and multiculturalism, that threaten a sense of sameness, identity, and way of life (Stenner & Haidt, 2018). Within far-right movements, the sense is that "others," ranging from Obama, Democrats, socialists, and even child-murdering pedophiles, are taking over, and it is increasingly certain that "this is not my government … These are not my people" (p. 176). Authoritarian populist leaders foment polarization along such lines in order to acquire power, and once this has been achieved, they further an exclusionary stance against those who "disagree with … [the leader as] … the supposedly authentic representative of the people" (Müller, 2021, p. 9).

One of this country's preeminent twentieth-century historians, Richard Hofstadter, offered in his seminal thesis (1965) an understanding of the *paranoid style* long operative in the American polity, in which there is a particular affinity for bad (rather than good) causes. It seems compelling that during times of acute and excessive political anxiety, as manifest in the period after the 9/11 attacks and during President Obama's tenure, an angry authoritarian temperament marked by paranoid tendencies is apt to arise from the insecurities and social rootlessness, the *normative threats* of recent transformations in American life. As noted, when environmental conditions are perceived as existentially threatening, the predisposition to authoritarianism is activated, both in individuals and groups. Moreover, economic self-interest is not the major factor accounting for this fervor, instead, we must look more deeply at unconscious, less rational dynamics in play that have helped to create today's substantial cultural schism. Cultural wars that took hold in the late 1980s and early 1990s have led to divisions that are now less ideological, instead being far more visceral, aggressive, and tribal.[3]

[3] Whereas the term *identity politics* is sometimes applied to an effort to demonstrate that one belongs to the *real people*, it actually refers to the particular form of political activism linked to cultural identities that "is about claiming that basic rights have to be made effective" (Müller, 2021, p. 77).

Hofstadter—undoubtedly influenced by the Frankfurt School's critical theorizing pertaining to the forces of politics and ideological movements that are bound up with the unconscious workings of individual psyches expressed in support of the group dynamic—made it clear in describing the *paranoid style* that he was not speaking as a clinician, but rather was describing a style of mind that has a long and varied history (Adorno, 1951; Adorno et al., 1950; Löwenthal & Guterman, 1949). This style of mind is a *way of seeing the world* and is characterized by heated exaggeration, suspiciousness, and conspiratorial fantasy, all of which contribute to *persecutory feelings* and systematized, *grandiose conspiracy theories*. Within the group, then, the hostile, conspiratorial world is imagined to be directed against a way of life, a culture, or even a nation. The central preoccupation of the paranoid style is typically the purported existence of a secretive and "vast, insidious preternaturally effective international conspiratorial network" (Hofstadter, 1965, p. 14), designed to perpetrate fiendish acts to destroy a treasured way of life or a nation.

In brief, the paranoid style is distinguished by a "vast" or "gigantic" conspiracy, typically described in apocalyptic terms, which seeks to undermine and destroy a way of life and serves as the motivating force in historical events. In line with Christian themes in which there is a spiritual wrestling match between *absolute good* and *absolute evil*, apocalyptic warnings arouse passion and militancy, and as such, they often appeal to fundamentalist, evangelical Christians operating in a prophetic cult. In what is fundamentally *Manichean psychology*, compromise is eschewed, and what is perceived as necessary is to fight to a finish in which the only acceptable outcome is nothing less than complete victory over a clearly delineated, malicious enemy. That enemy—often representing a projection of idealized and unacceptable aspects of the self (i.e., the selves of individual members)—is viewed as possessing an especially effective source of power, while also conceived of as a "perfect model of malice … sinister, ubiquitous, powerful, cruel, sensual, luxury-loving" (ibid., pp. 32–33). In fact, such thinking often incorporates an obsession with sadistic details—such as in today's QAnon conspiratorial theories, which include the idea that anti-Trumpist democrats and liberal elites are part of a cabal of Satan-worshipping, cannibalistic pedophiles running a global child sex-trafficking ring.

Such conspiracy theories have taken hold at the extremes of this populist movement, while increasingly becoming manifest in mainstream political thought as well. Conspiratorial thinking has been studied by interdisciplinary researchers from the fields of social and political psychology, sociology, political science history, and the humanities; for example, an extremely comprehensive review details research led by UK social psychologist Karen Douglas (Douglas et al., 2019).

In examining her team's empirical findings, Douglas and colleagues note that conspiracy beliefs are most prevalent at political extremes, and while occurring among both the far left and the far right, they tend to be stronger on the right. Consistent with both Adorno's (1967) and Hofstadter's (1965) seminal writings, Douglas finds that conservatives appear more likely to accept such theories than are liberals.[4] Arguably, then, there seems to be "a link between conspiracy beliefs and right-wing authoritarianism"—perhaps because right-wingers are "more likely to exhibit the personality predispositions that foster conspiracy thinking, such as the need to manage uncertainty" (Douglas et al., 2019, p. 11; see also Applebaum, 2020; Stenner, 2005; Stenner & Haidt, 2018).

Conspiracy theories seek to describe ultimate causes or agendas and typically involve social, cultural, and political events and conditions in which two or more formidable actors are alleged to be engaged in a secret plot. In general, the existence of the purported conspiracy may or may not be evidentially provable; it may be propagated for a variety of reasons, some of which may be socially beneficial, though most are likely to be problematic.

As suggested in my discussion of the authoritarian predisposition and its activation under conditions of so-called normative threat, research findings suggest that certain people or groups are especially drawn to conspiracy theories, and in line with my thesis, the attraction is often based on existential or social factors. For some individuals, "cultural despair," in which an identity once widely shared—as, for example,

---

[4] Linda Greenhouse (2021), a Pulitzer Prize-winning legal journalist, contends that a persecutory narrative manifests even among the most elite Republican conservatives, such as Supreme Court Justice Samuel Alito. She refers to this *grievance conservatism* as a veritable cult of victimhood in which very privileged Americans believe they are being unfairly deprived *even when* they are actually profiting from their higher status.

that of white supremacy—is experienced as stolen and replaced with something inferior. Some turn to these theories when they believe their *existential needs* are threatened; thus, such beliefs are associated with feelings of powerlessness, anxious attachment styles, and alienation from the prevailing political system.

Social scientists argue that, overall, a belief in such theories is more likely to be found among people who are essentially less able to engage in analytic, critical thinking, perhaps resulting from a lack of cognitive tools (which may in turn relate to a lack of education) that enable more flexible and less binary forms of thought. However, as psychoanalysis reminds us, the capacity to tolerate uncertainty and not knowing—what Bion (1970) refers to as *negative capability*—is tied to unconscious emotional functioning and tends to represent a developmental achievement. Nonetheless, using conspiratorial theories to assign blame to others in an attempt to enhance self-worth and virtue—especially in the simplicity and either-or reasoning of this approach—is emotionally appealing to those predisposed to authoritarianism for a variety of reasons, in that the believer gains a "sense of having special, privileged access to the truth" (Applebaum, 2020, p. 45).

Other important research from another perspective was conducted by Shauna Bowes and her team at Emory University (Bowes et al., 2021), who completed an extensive analysis of personality characteristics among individuals prone to hold conspiratorial beliefs. Bowes argued that the profiles most associated with such beliefs are immodest entitlement, self-centered impulsivity, a sense of being wronged, and heightened levels of depressive and anxious moods. At the extreme, the researchers found milder forms of paranoid ideation and a form of thinking termed *psychoticism* (though this was not prevalent).

It is particularly concerning, as Douglas et al. (2019) have noted, that such beliefs are often linked to violent intentions and reactions in situations of threat. A case in point is *dominant group status threat*, in which group members are in danger of being at the losing end of the power hierarchy; here we find increased likelihood of a strong group attachment that fosters conspiracy beliefs potentially leading to radicalization and extremist, even at times violent behavior. This phenomenon may help us understand something about the minds of those who actively perpetrated the January 6, 2021 insurrection at the US Capitol. When a group thinks of itself as under threat as well as undervalued and deprived, the conviction that others are conspiring against the group is intensified.

We might ask *how* conspiratorial thinking emerges among such populist groups. An interesting, historically based model has been offered by Sophia Rosenfeld (2019). In the first stage, unjustly powerless "real people" are exalted, assuaging their feeling of betrayal by elites (such as liberals, politicians, bankers, academics, and Jews). Presenting themselves as champions of democracy, these self-identified "real people" thereby disguise the populist group's exclusionary opposition to pluralism and perhaps to liberal democracy itself (Müller, 2021). Gripes about their powerlessness tend to morph into a full-blown conspiracy theory starring the "unjustifiably powerful" (S. Rosenfeld, 2019, p. 99), such as "swamp-dwelling" politicians and officials in the "deep state." Finally, the process concludes in a fairytale-like denouement that reflects a new, more mythic social role for the *real* people—such as their participation in "draining the swamp" and being restored to an imagined, nostalgic sense of greatness.

To reiterate, this process has taken hold among Trump supporters and is most evident in QAnon's conspiratorial notion of Democratic Party-run child pornography rings. However, the process itself is nothing new, and as Hofstadter (1965) delineated, this strain of extremist, paranoid thinking along *conspiratorial lines* has long resided in the American polis; it is a style particularly evident among the right wing (though neither unique to the US nor absent from the left wing). Hofstadter noted that the paranoid style tends to be linked with movements of suspicious discontent—often as a common ingredient of *fascism* and frustrated *nativism* and *nationalism*. It represents "an old and recurrent mode of expression in our public life" (ibid., p. 6), though it tends to take precedence only among "minority movements" (p. 7), while seeming to be ineradicable. Somewhat presciently, Hofstadter observed that among paranoid groups, a *Manichean political psychology* often converges with prevailing *cultural (and identity) politics*, along with *anti-intellectualism*, to produce such extreme phenomena among radical *pseudo-conservatives*.

To further contextualize the rise of destructive populism in the US today, it is useful to note that in his essay of more than a half century ago, Hofstadter noted that, throughout US history, there have been numerous largely right-wing conspiratorial and populist movements seeking to counter the putative threats posed by certain groups. These out-groups have been viewed as bent on destroying American civilization and the favored group's or caste's way of life. Following are some specific examples: the *anti-Masonic* (and *anti-Illuminati*) movement, seen by its proponents as countering reputed Masonic destruction of Christianity by massive libertinism in the eighteenth and nineteenth centuries; *nativist, anti-Catholic*, and *anti-Mormon* movements in the nineteenth century; the largely *anti-Jewish international bankers and munitions makers* in the late nineteenth and early twentieth centuries; Joseph McCarthy's *anti-Communist* movement in the mid-twentieth century; and various *white supremacist, anti-black segregationist* movements beginning in the eighteenth century and continuing to the present day (e.g., the Ku Klux Klan, American Nazi Party, John Birch Society, Aryan Brotherhood, Boogaloo Movement, Michigan Militia, Oath Keepers, Three Percenters, and Proud Boys).

The rise of paranoid ideation

These groups have sought to counter various threatening conspiracy plots purportedly perpetrated by white liberals, abolitionists, people of color, etc.—plots that, if left unchecked, would lead to black Americans raping (or attracting) white women while replacing and eliminating white men. Ideologically similar anti-Muslim, anti-Latino, and anti-immigrant movements have singled out non-white Americans and labeled them terrorists, rapists, murderers, and destroyers of "what made America great." Finally, long-standing and still extant anti-Semitism in the US (reflected in a conspiratorial book dating from the early twentieth century, *The Protocols of the Elders of Zion*) has promoted the belief that prominent Jews in banking, education, entertainment, and science are allegedly seeking world domination.

Hofstadter set the stage for our better understanding of the cult-like features of destructive populism, the operation of paranoid mindedness, and the role of a malignant narcissistic leader. In *the paranoid mind* of extreme groupings (what analysts might describe as the group's residing in the paranoid–schizoid [P/S] position), a crusading and conspiratorial mentality holds that all societal ills can be traced to a single evil source that must be eliminated by a final act of victory that vanquishes evil and prevents an apocalyptic result. Although elements of truth and reality inevitably contribute to conspiratorial delusions (as is the situation in clinical paranoia), what stands out in the group's paranoid style is the *absolutist and apocalyptic framework* in which hostility to the evil other (group) or selected villain is expressed, and a single hostile force represented by a large group must be struggled against with a sustaining sense of grandeur and destiny.

Hofstadter's greatest contribution may have been in observing how such paranoid, conspiratorial thinking can mix its fortune with American party politics. In revelatory fashion more than a half century ago, describing what might be understood today as a large swath of Trump's Republican base, he noted that the "modern right wing … feels dispossessed … [in that] America has been largely taken away from them and their kind" (p. 23). Long before the internet and the impact of social media, Hofstadter presciently posited that important changes could be traced to the effects of mass media (largely television and print media at that time).

Furthermore, in what can be seen as a prelude to today's alt-right extremism evident in the MAGA organization and Trumpism's conspiratorial assault on the "deep state" and its democratic structure, Hofstadter stated that "[O]ld American virtues have … been eaten away by *cosmopolitans and intellectuals*; … old competitive capitalism has been gradually undermined *by socialist and communist schemers*; and … old national security and independence have been destroyed by treasonous plots … [by] their most powerful agents [being] … major *statesmen seated at the very centers of American power*" (pp. 23–24, italics added).

In the group's imaginative fantasies, these allegedly evil statesmen supposedly pave the way for the rise of socialism or communism by bringing the US economy "under the direction of the federal government" (p. 25), so that today's "demonic" forces are easily thought of as led by Nancy Pelosi, Chuck Schumer, Kamala Harris, AOC, and the squad—all of whom began as offshoots of "the foreign-born, fake" president: Barack *Hussein* Obama.

In the next chapter, I consider how Trump has uniquely managed to access and utilize these elements in a particularly destructive fashion; I then outline salient psychoanalytic ways of understanding such psychotic group processes. In short, I aim to clarify how we might better understand how Trump and Trumpism captivate so many decent and otherwise democratically oriented Americans.

CHAPTER 3

Psychoanalytic perspectives on destructive populism and large-group regression: the rise of Trumpism in the US

There's something happening here
But what it is ain't exactly clear

There's a man with a gun over there
A-telling me, I got to beware …

Paranoia strikes deep
Into your life it will creep

It starts when you're always afraid
Step out of line, the man come and take you away …

We better stop, hey, what's that sound
Everybody look what's going down

—"For What It's Worth," by Stephen Stills
Recorded by Buffalo Springfield (1966)

How is it that a destructive, narcissistic leader such as Donald Trump can garner and maintain a tenacious hold on a large segment of the

American population? Arguably, this becomes a "fatal destructive fit between group and leader," one that produces fundamental *attacks against "liberal, pluralistic, and triangulating structures"* (Zienert-Eilts 2020, p. 977, italics added). Can a psychoanalytic perspective help us better understand how Trump and Trumpism captivate so many decent and otherwise democratically oriented Americans?

Trump's populistic appeal: attacks on consensual reality and the ideals of democracy

Trump has appealed to the *popular masses*' long-standing hostility toward the *elites* (Packer, 2021a) by assigning to a *partisan, leftist agenda* such historically bipartisan issues as *science, public health safety* (e.g., mask wearing, social distancing, and COVID-19 vaccinations), *legal vote counts, cultural diversity,* and *international diplomacy*—all of which were once undisputedly supported by both political parties. Thus, domination by those in a self-interested caste who promote themselves as the sole truth tellers has assumed prominence and must be battled against by the *real people,* whose articulated enemies include professors, journalists, think-tankers, Wall Street leaders, scientists, international health experts, trade negotiators, and the overall "liberal elites" represented by the mainstream press and media (e.g., *The New York Times, The Washington Post,* CNN, MSNBC, etc.).

Despite the fact that many Americans have long been convinced that liberal democracy is irreversible, the country's founders were not so certain and believed that special measures were essential "to prevent democracy from sliding back into tyranny" (Applebaum, 2020, p. 142). As I will elaborate, Trump's rise to power and his cult of personality have exposed unresolvable divisions that far too many Americans have not been particularly aware of. Applebaum, the author just quoted, is a self-described long-standing member of the conservative Republican elites (who include Max Boot, David Brooks, David Frum, Bill Kristol, and John Podhoretz, among others), yet she rues the fact that Trump's authoritarian attacks on democracy have taken hold of the Republican Party in Trump's America. Here a form of moral equivalence rooted in deep right-wing pessimism, nativism, and nationalism holds that there is no important distinction between democracy and dictatorship.

As Applebaum notes, "The unity of this America is created by white skin, a certain idea of Christianity, and attachment to land that will be surrounded and defended by a wall" (2020, p. 158).

However, the ideals of the democratic truth process—*a shared version of reality*—had been severely threatened even prior to Trump's brazen trading in misinformation, lying, and bullshit. For instance, consider the role played over the last four decades by individuals and entities such as Gingrich, Rove, Fox News, Rupert Murdoch, the Koch Brothers, and the Mercer Family Foundation, among many others (see, for example, Acemoglu & Robinson, 2020; Applebaum, 2020; Fishkin, 2018; Levitsky & Ziblatt, 2018; MacLean, 2017; Müller, 2021; Packer, 2021b; S. Rosenfeld, 2019; Zelizer, 2020). Consequently, in view of the populist backlash created against what has been (or seemingly has been) a monopoly of public policy by experts, the prevailing issue becomes a question: Who gets to say what is true?

Tragically, in the currently polarized approach to truth, there is a binary answer: *either* the experts *or* the people (S. Rosenfeld, 2019). In this environment in which *truth* is a shadowy term, Trump advisors speaking on NBC's time-honored program *Meet the Press*, such as Kellyanne Conway (in 2017), can say without blinking an eye that "There are alternative truths," and Rudy Giuliani (in 2018) can unashamedly declare that "Truth isn't truth." Given the role played by revolutionary changes in technology and communications, such as the impact of social media algorithms encouraging false perception and disinformation, arguments and differences of opinion based on "agreed parameters" within a common narrative have largely vanished; instead, we are now dealing with different facts and alternative realities, and despite verifiable fact checking, "[T]here is no easy way to distinguish between *conspiracy theories* and *true stories*" (Applebaum, 2020, p. 113, italics added).

Steve Bannon, the ideological force behind Trump's rise to political office, orchestrated an exploitation of paranoid, conspiratorial theories about elites, liberals, leftists, blacks, and immigrants. In addition, he called upon hand-picked "experts" in an effort to destroy long-standing democratic institutions and norms. By skillfully using the right-wing media machine (e.g., Breitbart, Fox News) and by targeting social media (e.g., Facebook, Twitter) in ways that have exploited the country's divisive fault lines, Trump's strategists mounted a campaign that leftist detractors were ill prepared to cope with. The right wing's ruthless threats of violence were rarely matched on the left (Shapiro, 2020).

By touting his self-proclaimed instinctual "genius" cultivated in the "real" world of business and commerce, Trump positioned himself as the "outsider coming in to bring ... people-based truth to the byzantine ways of Washington" (S. Rosenfeld, 2019, p. 127). In appealing to his base, he signals in a contradictory way that while he is "one of them, he is also a special person ... uniquely suited to lead them" (Loewenstein, 2020, p. 49). He declared himself the "stable genius" who would "drain the swamp" and added, "I alone can fix it."

But Trump's megalomaniacal proclamations alone would be insufficient without the aid of his enablers, acolytes, and sycophants, such as Sean Hannity, Rush Limbaugh, Tucker Carlson, Laura Ingraham, Fox News, Alex Jones, One American News (OAN), Newsmax, etc.—all of whom adeptly help to further divide the American people by broadening the warring gap between populists/Trumpists and those who do not support Trump. As a charismatic populist demagogue, Trump has captured a large share of the media, including that portion that serves to denounce him (this remains so even after his suspension from Facebook, Instagram, and Twitter). Moreover, as is inevitably the case with authoritarian, proto-fascist leaders, the crucial decisions that help empower such demagogues tend to be made by the current and prevailing "conservative establishment" elites, who collaborate to undermine democracy by taking the uncertainty out of elections through propaganda about "voter fraud," ruthless gerrymandering, and voter suppression that reduces the participation of the potential opposition (Müller, 2021).[1]

It is noteworthy that this more radical, authoritarian extremism is particularly dangerous in America's two-party system; in contrast to the US, in many other countries with democratically based political systems there are several parties (as is the case in some European nations, for example), so that the tendency is for a smaller faction of the population to be represented by the extreme of the polity. In short, the threat to democracy in the US is particularly acute when a radical, authoritarian

---

[1] Jan-Werner Müller (2021) examined the rise of fascism under Hitler and concluded that "[I]t is not the people who decide to be done with democracy; it is the elites" (p. xi).

faction takes over one of the two essential political parties (Levitsky & Ziblatt, 2018; see also Woodward & Costa, 2021).

In consequence of these and other factors, rather than there being a respectful and historically more democratically based *battle of ideas* between parties equally committed to democratic norms and ideas, primitive anxieties and rage are continually stoked. As a response to poorly contained tensions and increasing perceptions of traumatizing levels of threat, large group regression becomes more likely. Hence a populist takeover of the Republican Party has become apparent, and with it a "de facto disappearance of the ... loyal opposition" (Müller, 2021, p. 68). Both sides of the increasing divide are relieved of the democratic imperative to persuade based on truthful, consensual reality—and meaningful dialogue or debate is precluded. In this polarized atmosphere, Hannity, Ingraham, and Carlson of Fox News trade in blatantly false hyperbole, whereas MSNBC's Rachel Maddow falls prey at times to a provocatively snarky campaign against the mendacity, albeit devoid of sufficient understanding or compassion for those who cling to "alternative" truths. Hence, to reiterate, more traditionally nonpartisan and venerable issues—such as public health and safety during a national health crisis, scientific facts, legally conducted elections, social diversity, and international diplomacy—are too easily rendered part of a leftist propaganda agenda contributing to a destructive form of populism.

In order to better understand how Trump and his followers have managed to adroitly twist and debauch the necessary foundations of nonmalignant normality, I will utilize the lens of psychoanalysis to explore American forms of populism, including how it turns destructive through regressive mechanisms in large groups.

Authoritarian populism through a psychoanalytic lens

As noted in Chapter 2, the conditions leading to Trump's election and the rise of his personality cult, *Trumpism*, were created over the course of several decades. Especially important was the transformation of power and identity after the unprecedented attacks of September 11, 2001, as evidenced in both the concentration of power in the executive branch and the erosion of rights and liberties in the service of "security." Trump then enters the stage as an aspiring autocrat who fits socially oriented psychoanalyst Erich Fromm's (1964) characterization of a demagogue appealing to the people's vision of an imaginary past by conveying that he's "the only one" who can take the country back—so that, as Trump's campaign slogan promised, America could be "made great again."

In applying specifically psychoanalytic thinking to the phenomenon of populism, Zienert-Eilts (2020) distinguishes *general populism*, which utilizes populist methods characterized by slogans, from *destructive populism*, which uses populist methods to promote destructive contents and goals that target negative affect in the masses. She notes that these targeted negative affects pertain to deep-seated and terrifying fears, persecutory feelings, envy, primitive aggression, and splitting through polarizing divisions. Interdependence is denied and cultural wars are waged based on a stoked-up fear of "losing the country." The ambient societal zeitgeist is one in which "a virtuous and homogenous" group is pitted against elites and dangerous others who are "trying to deprive them of their rights, values, prosperity, identity, and voice" (Stenner & Haidt, 2018, p. 178). Consequently, and consistent with the thinking of historians, the prevailing attitudes within destructive populism are: (a) *anti-elitism*; (b) *anti-pluralism*; and (c) the claiming of *sole moral representation*.

When a group becomes dominated by terrifying existential threats, its members seek the certitude of what is known rather than the uncertainty of the unknown. The group's narcissistic tendencies become more activated and can easily dominate, so that primitive, less developmentally mature (i.e., regressive) levels of psychic functioning stimulate defensive processes—such as splitting and projective identification—that are relied upon to eliminate threatening differences. In the vulnerable, regressed group psyche that seeks to return to tension-free functioning, an *us-versus-them* dynamic is created in which the *other* is demonized and perceived as dangerous to the group's survival. In examining such large-group regression, Fromm (1964) suggested that, under threat, a type of *group or collective narcissism* surfaces that reflects the group's grandiosity or greatness, opposing the out-group's failure to acknowledge the in-group's superiority while strengthening members' attachment to the group. In response to feeling helpless, the "group self's" narcissistic rage tends to escalate (Wolf, 1988). Moreover, in political groupings, conspiracy theories arise more frequently when markedly uncomfortable psychological states—such as feelings of powerlessness, escalating uncertainty, and unpredictability, as well as low political trust fueling alternative beliefs—are stimulated, especially by malignant leaders.

When populism turns destructive

Very few psychoanalytic writers have examined populism's destructive potential from a psychoanalytic perspective—though, as noted, more recently, several analysts (such as Chrzanowski, 2019) have employed Bion's group concept of basic assumptions; Kernberg (2020) discussed his thinking about malignant narcissism primarily in relation to Freud and to Bion's work on groups; and Zienert-Eilts (2020) applied Bion's containing paradigm in conjunction with H. Rosenfeld's concept of destructive narcissism.

As suggested in Chapter 2, populism itself is not inherently destructive and is often useful in a democracy in its logic and success as a narrative addressing problematic issues. However, historians maintain that it is clearly unsuccessful as a "style of governance" (S. Rosenfeld, 2019, p. 135). Furthermore, it is of significant concern when a charismatic leader such as Trump, with his autocratic posturing, becomes capable of bringing together diverse factions of populist extremes, as he has—factions who then manage to seriously threaten democracy by their attacks on verifiable truth, eradication of standards and norms, and exacerbation of real problems through development of weak or bad policies.

Again, it is plainly evident in the behavior of Trump's supporters that destructive forms of populism are apt to be directed against the structures and traditions of representative democracy as determined by the separation of powers—particularly the free press and independent judiciary. Attacks on democracy, which fundamentally encompasses plurality and uncertainty, can arise from the left or the right, reflecting what has been termed *demophobia*—namely, a fear of ordinary people (across the political spectrum) who tend to be demonized and viewed as a threat to one's own group's survival. Trumpism thrives on rendering the opposition as socialist, elitist leftists seeking to take away the freedoms that "made America great." Demophobia also arises among anti-Trumpists who regard Trump supporters as "deplorable," second-class citizens. Müller (2021) notes that such suspicion of the masses in the form of fearing a wave of unstoppable authoritarianism presents the danger of re-empowering traditional elites to serve as gatekeepers who might override democratic norms. For example, we have seen how many Congressional Republicans, aware that there is no verifiable evidence that the 2020 election was "stolen," and surely believing that the January 6, 2021 Capitol insurrection requires serious bipartisan investigation, have opted either to remain silent or to actively obstruct the truth. The degradation of democracy is then justified in order to prevent imagining something far worse, such as a governmental takeover by "far-left socialists." In particular, having interviewed more than 200 individuals at the center of the insider turmoil, acclaimed Washington journalists Bob Woodward and Robert Costa (2021) recently documented how such activities have offered a compelling portrait of a nation on the brink.

Zienert-Eilts (2020), applying Kernberg's (2020) insights, Bion's (1961, 1962) container/contained paradigm, and H. Rosenfeld's (1987) concept of *destructive narcissism*, argues that populist-dominated groups are susceptible to regression to the paranoid–schizoid position, in which "aggressively destructive and omnipotent affects are idealized and the container function of democratic society is increasingly decomposed, distorted, and finally twisted" (p. 971). As briefly noted in Chapter 2, when liberal democracy's necessary tensions cannot be sufficiently tolerated or contained by either or both sides of the essential dialectic through a commitment to its core tenets and norms, *extreme group regression* is likely to develop in response to perceived existential threats. Interestingly, the three planks delineated by Zienert-Eilts (2020) seem to characterize the strategically divisive methodology of Stephen Bannon (who, as noted, initially served as the chief ideologist in Trump's populist movement), which is characterized by: (1) anti-elitism; (2) anti-permanent political class; and (3) anti-consolidation of media and technology.

Kleinian thinking, as elaborated by Bion, Jaques, Bleger, and Herbert Rosenfeld, laid the foundation for understanding complex destructive processes in groups. Hence Bion's (1962) paradigm of a *container*, Bleger's (1967) *frame*, and Volkan's (2004) and Kernberg's (2020) *second skin* can be applied to constructive and destructive social (group) processes. Furthermore, H. Rosenfeld's (1984, 1987) work on primitive narcissistic object relations indicates more specific totalitarian intrapsychic processes and destructive structures that operate "like a Mafia gang";

in other words, a system is created in which good and evil are reversed, and narcissistic omnipotence and brutality are idealized. In this more psychotic domain, what is good, compassionate, and considerate is perverted into something weak and despicable; by the same token, what is evil, destructive, cruel, and autocratic is regarded as strong, admirable, and idealized.

In short, then, there are a number of shared characteristics in the regressively destructive populist mode in which narcissism, omnipotence, and psychotic disavowal predominate; these include: (1) idealization of primitive omnipotent destructive aspiration; (2) projection of one's own destructive aggression and envy onto immigrants, women, independent others, and social activists (e.g., those of the Black Lives Matter movement); (3) perversion in the form of reversal of good and evil, truth and lying; and (4) attacks against libidinous connections (e.g., LGBTQ), triangulating structures (e.g., democratic checks and balances; the concept of the symbolic/paternal third), and independent, individualized (critical) thinking. H. Rosenfeld (1984) and later Kernberg (2020) went further to illuminate the seductively perverse relational dynamics between an autocrat or dictator and the approving masses operating within a destructive populist social structure.

In order to better appreciate how a malignant leader and destructive populism coalesce, it is necessary to clarify what is meant by *psychotic thinking* and its manifestation within larger groups.

Populism, destructive social processes, and regressive psychotic processes in large groups

As implied in Chapter 2, Adorno's (1967) seminal work on authoritarianism and extremism, which was influential in the development of Hofstadter's (1965) ideas about the paranoid style in American politics, suggests similarities between *right-wing extremism* and the structures of *destructive populism* that attack democracy's stabilizing institutions, configurations, and traditions, all of which serve to limit power and encourage communication. A comprehension of extremist thinking was furthered by Erich Fromm (1955, 1964), who took up the role played by *narcissism* in malignant large groups, including nations. For instance, he described narcissism in groups as involving the transference (and projection) to the large group or nation of individual members' omnipotent overestimation of their own position and a hatred for all who differ from it—as seen, for example, in the belief that they are saving their country or area (be it Nazi Germany or the segregationist Southern US) from its impending destruction (by Jews or blacks, respectively). From a different analytic perspective, Era Loewenstein (2018) suggests that the rigid structures holding together the fragile core of regressed groups requires a constant supply of malevolent enemies in order to consolidate and maintain the group's grandiose, paranoid, and perverse features.

Most germane to my thesis, Fromm (1964) wrote that under these circumstances, extreme group narcissism often becomes malignant by giving rise to fanaticism, dangerous illusions, and fascist politics. He posited that the working classes are particularly susceptible to what became apparent as the racial narcissism of Hitler's Germany and of the segregationist South in the US. In considering the symbiotic connection between such groups and their leaders, Fromm suggested that groups whipped up into a narcissistic fervor are eager to find a fanatical, narcissistic leader with whom to identify; "the greater the leader … the greater the follower" (p. 76), he adds.

In examining populism in the United States, Hoffman (2018) contends that Appalachian and Rust Belt working-class whites who are most susceptible to replacement-based existential threats are particularly vulnerable to populist appeals to denounce outsider groups—especially when encouraged by a leader like Trump, who reinforces the need to "fight" in order to preserve the country. Consequently, a "fight-flight" basic assumption process takes form in the larger regressed group.

Most recently, as will be discussed further in what follows, Kernberg (2020) has addressed the regressive facets of larger-group dynamics and the role played by malignant, narcissistic leadership. Moreover, in recognizing the mutual identifications found in such groups, Volkan (2020) notes that for a large group in a regressed state, "[T]he personality and the internal world of *the political leader* assume great importance concerning the manipulation (the 'good' or the 'bad') of what already exists within the large group psychology" (p. 46, italics added). According to both Volkan (2004, 2020) and Kernberg (2020), the regressed group requires a leader to provide a *second skin* to recover a lost sense of existential security that had been protected by social structures assuring its members of their individualized identities (i.e., largely their status and role relationships).

Essential psychoanalytic contributions have recently been made by several contemporary American psychoanalysts, including Bollas (2018, 2020), Loewenstein (2018), Hoffman (2013), Chrzanowski (2019), Kernberg (2020), and Volkan (2004, 2020), as well as German analyst Zienert-Eilts (2020). For example, Bollas (2018, 2020) stresses the disturbed psychological processes operative in thought and action that can easily occur in large groups, such as nations. He focuses on the collapse of social structures crucial to large-group functioning, which creates a psychotic social reality in which *law* no longer operates to control what he calls "id capitalism," in which greed and individual acquisition of "freedoms" exceed normal social constraints and regulation. When this occurs, property is privileged over persons and pleasure is favored over people—for instance, in attacks on mask wearing and social distancing.

In positing the new normal as a situation of *anarcho-capitalism* that results from successful attacks on the regulatory benefits of government, Bollas (2020) suggests that we are seeing a form of massive psychopathy marked by an unconscious strategy for gaining immediate gratification without consideration of consequences. This represents a *killing* or annihilation of the conscientious self, resulting in the death of crucial human qualities; unfiltered sadistic tendencies are then easily released, as evident in slogans such as "kill the protestors," "kidnap the governors," "lock them (her/him) up," and "hang Mike Pence." In line with a phenomenon described by Jaques, Bleger, and Herbert Rosenfeld, the mad, psychotic element is released and the sane, healthy parts remain more quiescent (or perhaps "evacuated").

Bollas describes the psychotic processes operative in contemporary Trumpist America, and in particular the evacuation of healthier, containing parts of the mind via projective identification processes that would ordinarily handle distressing thoughts. These evacuated, albeit needed mental structures are assigned to the leader, who serves as the *second skin* (Volkan; Kernberg), the *container* (Bion), or the *ego ideal* (Freud). In line with the earlier described thinking about the paranoid, conspiratorial style inherent in American politics, the regressive large group's psychotic process attempts to eliminate intrapsychic conflict by *denying* mental conflicts and *splitting* the collective self, so that unwanted parts are banished by being projected into a demonized other (i.e., malignant othering). This in turn produces fear of the other's revenge and a paranoid retreat into enclaves of supporters, often while operating within a *delusional system* evident in conspiracy theories.

Moreover, Trump's lying (and/or "bullshitting") has too rarely been understood as existing along a *psychotic spectrum* in which reality perception is constantly being revised. Consequently, a *psychotic mythopoesis* sucks Americans into such a mental process, which arguably suggests a psychotic-like hatred for the awareness of reality (Bollas, 2020).

Because the psychotic group process involves destruction of important, developmentally mature mental functions (e.g., reality perception, executive functioning, affect management, social adaptability), group members unconsciously experience the loss of these parts as evidence of the self's having been invaded and diminished by the enemy (for example, by Nancy Pelosi, AOC, Bernie Sanders, and the liberal elite, as well as by socialist and Jewish leftists such as George Soros). Faith-based thinking, particularly in the group's leader, comes to replace reasoning, and reasoned arguments are displaced by convictions.

In another interesting psychoanalytic approach, Chrzanowski (2019) characterizes such large-group regression—among both Trump supporters and his detractors—as emerging from Bion's (1961) idea of the *basic assumption group*, especially the idea that the group is a part-object of the mother's body that defends against psychotic anxieties loaded "towards the disordered, psychotic, uncanny, and inanimate" (p. 718). Chrzanowski suggests that activated basic assumptions in populist groupings reflect an unconscious fantasy that can be omnipotently achieved, easily and effortlessly, "without any change, negotiation, or strain" (p. 712).

Through the group's *pairing assumption*, a leader is sought/created to save it from conflicts and despair by ushering in a "future unlike any other" (p. 713). The more unstructured the group is (and less work-group dominated), the more it searches for a boundary control function—namely, a leader in the form of a *container* (Bion, 1962) or *second skin* (Kernberg, 2020; Volkan, 2020). Consequently, in the regression occurring among Trump's base, regressive and dissociative tendencies related to *pairing group activity* meet the group's unconscious basic assumption in the promise of a Messiah, and indeed, "Trump alone will fix it"—that is, he will vanquish the socialists who are out to destroy our way of life, and he will "make America great again."

Psychoanalytic perspectives on large-group regression

Contributing to interdisciplinary ways of understanding large-group regressions, the unique contributions of psychoanalytic thinkers, particularly those well versed in Kleinian/Bionian theory, have taken up such existential matters in terms of more primordial, survival fears of being ejected from the maternal container (Ziener-Eilts, 2020), or as expressions of terrifying anxieties—either the anxiety of not acquiring, or that of losing—an essential *second skin* (Kernberg, 2020; Volkan, 2004). For instance, when traditional structures regulating daily life collapse, existential anxieties begin to permeate individuals whose lives are affected; consequently, a regressed large group is created that will require a *second skin* to serve as a new external structure that restores a sense of identity and security to the affected group (Volkan, 2020). The members of the regressed group idealize one another reciprocally through identification with an idealized leader, who possesses characteristics of malignant narcissism with significant paranoid features, ego syntonic aggression directed toward others, and antisocial behavior (Kernberg, 2020).

As discussed elsewhere in this book, the perfect storm of large-group regression coexisting with malignant leadership is most likely to occur when the socially inferior status of non-whites, immigrants, progressive leftists, socialists, and women among certain higher-ranking groups, predominantly men, Christians, orthodox Jews, and whites in general, tends to release fears of existential destruction and retribution by fantasized, imagined persecutors. When such terrifying paranoid–schizoid (P/S) anxieties take hold, obdurate leadership serves as an external structure—a second skin or container that promises illusory security, freedom, power, and moral superiority in an aspirational and utopian, tension-free group fantasy. Freud (1921) described this phenomenon as the unleashing of a form of irresponsibility unique to mass psychology.

Along these lines of thinking, more archaic fears and fantasies are fueled by increasing polarization between rich and poor, as well as by the gradual erosion of the omnipotence of certain long-established national and religious groups. In addition to these deeper existential and annihilating anxieties, such massive regression among those located higher up in the class structure—including power brokers, oligarchs, and wealthy capitalists motivated by avarice—might also involve *greedy and sadistic pleasures* in exploiting fears and regressive dynamics in order to maintain or further economic and class-based power in an atmosphere of "id capitalism" (Bollas, 2020).

Nonetheless, what has come to seem normal in contemporary American politics under the sway of Trumpism can be seen as a form of malignant normality, which I will briefly consider next.

American malignant normality

Trump's populism is at the apotheosis of *post-truth culture*, though it has been evolving over the last two to three decades, and it has vaulted us into the midst of a *national reality disorder* marked by malignant, regressive, and psychotic group processes (S. Rosenfeld, 2019). As I've indicated, this has been addressed by many historians and social scientists, as well as from converging angles by several psychoanalytic thinkers, such as Bollas (2020), Kernberg (2020), Lifton (2020), and Volkan (2020). Lifton (2020) put it succinctly: "There is no avoiding Donald Trump and the American version of malignant normality" (p. 423). Still, Trump is no Nazi, nor are most of his followers.[2] Nonetheless, he and they preside over a malignant normality that consists of falsehoods and lies, in addition to vicious attacks on honorable men and women because they have contested these falsehoods.

Such malignancy is also evident in the embrace of the lies of dictators such as Vladimir Putin, in the rejection of truths brought forward by American intelligence agencies about Putin's interference in the 2016 and 2020 elections, and in denial of the veracity of the 2020 election per se. It can also be seen in the undermining of American allies in their efforts at truth telling, and in the disdainful dismissal of COVID-19 as

---

[2] Award-winning journalist George Packer (2021b) argues that because Trump lacks an ideological program, he is undeserving of the term *fascist*. Instead, he is more aptly considered a *demagogue* in the "white nationalist" tradition: one who feeds on the hatred of elites (p. 113).

inconsequential—followed by the embrace of dangerous and false remedies and cures, as well as advocation of premature "liberation" from mitigating restraints, such as the wearing of masks, social distancing, and even medically validated vaccinations.

During the recently ended, four-year chaotic reign of malignant normality in which democratic norms, traditions, and standards have been under constant siege, Trump's strength was his unique fit with the group's regression—particularly in his persuasive cult-leader methodology (Chrzanowski, 2019) that mobilizes "the group's basic assumption mentalities" (p. 714). As the appointed leader who resides in the paranoid–schizoid position, he evokes an absence or deterioration of necessary, healthy alpha functioning and, consequently, his containing function is inherently perverted. Nonetheless, though his presidency has ended, Trump, a malevolent leader and perverted container, is "celebrated like a savior, promising to free his followers from feelings of hate, powerlessness, despair, and identity anxiety … [and], fatally, [as] a pretending, ostensibly understanding mother, and … [thus] an *allegedly* protective and omnipotent father is finally found" (Zienert-Eilts, 2020, p. 980, original italics).

In the next chapter, I will examine how more primitive, psychotic forms of functioning, as well as conspiratorial thinking within Trumpism, become dominant in the larger, regressed group. How is it that large-group dynamics and functioning can become fertile ground for paranoia and conspiratorial thinking?

CHAPTER 4

Psychotic processes, paranoia, and conspiratorial thinking in large groups

It is harder to focus on the danger of the common will,
the weaknesses of the human immune system, the ease
with which the toxins can infect succeeding generations.
Because it means the enemy, the threat, is not one man,
it is all of us, lurking in humanity itself.

—Isabel Wilkerson, "The Euphoria of Hate" in *Caste* (2020, p. 267)

In 1932, between the two World Wars, Freud (1933) corresponded with Albert Einstein in pursuit of greater understanding of the hatred and destructiveness manifested by war. In his letters, we can see that he admonished civilized societies to deal with the psychotic-level, primitive group processes somewhat hopefully through a "strengthening of the intellect" and "an internalization of the aggressive impulses" (p. 214). However, as suggested in Chapter 1 and addressed at length in Chapter 6, a rational approach involving strengthening the intellect and internalizing aggression cannot itself adequately regulate or contain the malignant, primitive forces operative in regressed large groups. Instead, we must come to a much deeper understanding of the dominant irrational, psychotic, and unconscious "mad" dynamics in play.

In order to apply such a psychoanalytic understanding to societal forces, it is useful to appreciate the correspondence between an individual's ability to regulate the more problematic, destructive aspects of his/her internal life, and the foundational principles of *constitutional, democratic societies* that require checks and balances of forces, given the sociopolitical, large-group context of uncertainty, threat, and desires for freedom and equality (Hoffman, 2018; see also Müller, 2021). Both in the individual psyche and the group psyche, defenses are mobilized to avoid the disturbing affect of fear or terror elicited by escalating uncertainty and threat. As suggested in Chapter 3, a psychoanalytic perspective, though not sufficient in itself, is especially helpful in addressing the inherent tensions and uncertainty that democracy requires. In our current sociopolitical environment, this is congruent with what psychoanalysis contends for both individuals and groups—namely, that the psyche (i.e., the ego) matures partly through recognizing and negotiating with uncertainty and lack.[1]

To elaborate more extensively on what I have discussed in Chapters 2 and 3, when aspects of external reality become unbearable as a result of their being too psychically threatening, such as the conviction of being annihilated, the self-preservative drive influences the ego to detach from that aspect of external reality in the effort to remain sane, both on an individual and a group basis (Freud, 1924a). This often produces an unconscious alliance with destructiveness and violence through a preponderance of vicious, annihilating impulses that operate through denial, disavowal, and splitting. For instance, in the *paranoid–schizoid position* (P/S), sanity is sought through an *omnipotent denial of psychic reality* (Klein, 1946); similarly, in an effort to negate awareness of reality,

---

[1] However, as noted in Chapter 2, the capacity to tolerate the tensions of uncertainty and not knowing—what Bion (1970) refers to as *negative capability*—is tied to unconscious emotional functioning and tends to represent a developmental achievement. When this is too difficult, as I will subsequently discuss, splitting defenses are utilized that take the form of *blaming* that which is external to the self. This might range from blaming the mother, to the world outside, or even God. Arguably, in the context of the democratic polity and group psychology, such blaming is often evident in rageful attacks on elites, on specific high-profile politicians, or on the government itself.

the psyche engages in *splitting off* part of the personality concerned with the awareness of internal and external reality (Bion, 1957). Typically, then, *disavowal* is used to omnipotently mitigate ideas posed by external reality (Rao, 2021). In Bion's conceptualization of traumatizing threat, desperate splitting (and related *projective identification*) produces a more perilous division between the psychotic (mad) and non-psychotic (sane) parts of the personality, resulting in attacks on the mental apparatus itself.

I will return to these ideas later in this chapter in discussing large-group functioning that utilizes delusional processes and cult-like methods. Let's turn next to a more general understanding of unconscious dynamics in regressed groups.

An overview of psychotic processes in regressed large groups

As noted in Chapter 3, the massive loss of a protective environment—a *second skin* or healthy *containing structure*—leads to powerful existential anxieties and initiates regressive functions (Kernberg, 2020). To restate this, the nature of regressed groups includes the attempt to attain a sense of power by mass mutual identification. This mutual identification provides a sense of safety, belonging, and control that results from being part of such a large group.

The group then tends to search for a leader with whom they can identify. Such a leader is perceived as powerful and, while feared, becomes idealized, and the regressed group manifests an almost complete identification with him/her. To reiterate, a leader with characteristics of paranoia and malignant narcissism offers the group powerful reassurance against its fears of loss both of status and of individual identity (Kernberg, 2020). Under these circumstances, however, the regressed large group functions in accordance with a more paranoid and narcissistic psychic organization, utilizing primitive defenses such as projection, introjection, splitting, avoidance, denial, primitive idealization and devaluation, and omnipotent control.

In Kleinian terms, the *paranoid–schizoid position* (P/S) predominates, and *projection*, *identification*, and *introjection* are used in a variety of ways. For instance, as Freud (1921) initially adumbrated, the group projects onto the leader an individualized ego ideal. Primitive idealization of Trump, for example, provides his followers with needed narcissistic supplies, and primitive devaluation of everything not-Trump provides his followers with objects deserving of vicious attacks. In the group's mass psychology, individual group members begin to feel free from moral restraint because the idealized leader now carries their omnipotent destructive impulses, which are sanctioned and perhaps glorified. The collective paranoid projections of aggression toward the enemy group produce a sense of internal goodness, which becomes a sense of entitlement, and then *denial* predominates in a gradual distortion of reality. This may easily lead to mob rule accompanied by violent action.

Through living in the paranoid–schizoid position, the group's members share a sense of equality, power, and freedom from moral constraints that heightens their acceptance of the leader's commands. This produces a realm of functioning that is more like that of a cult than a political movement that expresses an ideology, and thus a marker of large-group regression is a substantial diminution of rational, independent judgment (Kernberg, 2020; Lifton, 2020; see also Freud, 1921).

Consequently, the large group engages in *splitting* by idealizing the in-group (its adherents) and demonizing the out-group. A sharp division between *us* and *them* is established, and a sense of shared morality develops that becomes increasingly absolutist and punitive toward those who deviate even slightly from it. In effect, then, the group needs to operate through *disavowing*, *denying*, and *splitting off* conflictual aspects of reality; its members participate in a mass *negative hallucination* necessary to maintain the desperately needed experience of a protective second skin (Kernberg, 2020).

Moreover, partly to maintain the necessary *avoidance*, *disavowal*, and *denial*, the regressed group tends to focus on joint traumas and past triumphs, creating a time collapse in which past and present are confused. The group's "chosen trauma" is most likely a historical event in which its ancestors suffered catastrophic loss and humiliation at the hands of its enemies, yet there is no ability to mourn the loss (Volkan, 2020). For instance, among many Trump supporters, the Confederate flag represents not only the Civil War as experienced by the vanquished American South, but more implicitly signifies the loss of status suffered in attenuating white male superiority.

Before we examine through psychoanalytic lenses the roles played by destructive populism and psychotic malignancies that produce cultism in regressed large groups, it is useful to consider several insightful findings offered by social scientists that further explicate today's far-right populist, authoritarian wave.

The impact of fears and threats on large-group regression: perspectives complementary to that of psychoanalysis

As noted in Chapter 2, social scientists, particularly contemporary political scientists, historians, economists, and social psychologists, are interested in the *existential threat* to one's individual and group status. Demagogues thrive by exaggerating such threats; for instance, Trump evokes the affect of fear to promote divisive, non-empathic social interactions that further his acquisition and maintenance of power (Nussbaum, 2018). In addition, shifting demographics due to rising immigration rates and increasing numbers of non-native, non-white, "minority" Americans have led to the theory of *dominant group status threat* (Mutz, 2018). According to this view, a malaise of insecurities arises out of the sense that the out-group (i.e., ethnic and other minorities as well as immigrants) is doing "too well" and has become a viable threat to one's own dominant, white status. This is apparent in the fear seen among many whites of being replaced by the *other*, a fear largely stoked by a once-fringe, right-wing theory called the *Great Replacement*, which holds that minorities and immigrants are seeking to take over the country. For instance, consider a chant heard at the 2017 white supremacist "Unite the Right" rally in Charlottesville, Virginia: "Jews will not replace us!"

This phenomenon has also been seen as an indication of *racialized economics* (Sides et al., 2019), in which groups regarded as "undeserving" are seen to be "getting ahead," while one's own, more dominant group is left behind. Because of the perception of this (existential) threat, extreme measures are believed to be justifiable in order to restore to the "proper" people a sense of well-being and dominance. For instance, in a chilling yet sobering series of studies of over 400 insurrectionist rioters arrested for the January 6 attacks on the Capitol, political scientist Robert Pape and colleagues reported in 2021 that the driving factor among these mostly middle- to upper-middle-class white males was *not* economic anxieties, but rather replacement fears—in other words that their status would decline in the context of social changes (Pape & Ruby, unpublished).

In line with other social science-based findings, violent behavior was here driven largely by existential fears in which grievances, such as belief in a "stolen election," were fueled by agitating leadership from Trump and his acolytes. Unlike past right-wing extremists, most insurrectionists hailed from non-rural counties where non-white populations are growing fastest, very few are unemployed, and—most surprisingly—nearly half are of the white-collar and professional class, including doctors, lawyers, architects, portfolio managers, business owners, and governmental employees. The vast majority had no connection to far-right militias or groups such as the Oath Keepers, Proud Boys, or Three Percenters.

It is particularly disconcerting that among a nationally representative sample of the millions of mostly Republican voters who continue to believe that the 2020 election was "stolen," approximately 4 percent state that they are willing to engage in *violent* protest. Pape and his colleagues believe that this core insurrectionist base is growing among conservative Republicans (especially within its own media bubbles peopled by deceptive spokespersons and leaders). Thus, it is vital to persistently and speedily combat such polarizing narratives through recognition that the real driver of the propensity for violence is racially and caste-based *replacement fear*.

Even as we are forced to accept and take into account this intense replacement fear, what other factors might we identify as forming the motivations of the so-called base among Trump supporters? As noted in Chapter 2 (which I will subsequently expand upon to further incorporate interdisciplinary and psychoanalytic insights), latent authoritarian predispositions are more likely to become manifest in the context of perceived existential threats—termed *normative threats*—sparked by frightening societal conditions (Stenner, 2005; Stenner & Haidt, 2018). Moreover, as I've implied, prejudice on racial grounds is neither the primary motivation nor necessarily a fundamental motivating force; instead, clinging to racial identity occurs more in the service of protecting the group's collective interest in order to maintain their status.

It seems that the Republican Party has successfully rallied around its base, who are primarily members of a caste experiencing an existential threat to its status; and Trump, by channeling insecurities and disaffections (contra most more traditional Republicans) and by exploiting dominant group status threats and racialized economics, has skillfully stirred up passion among the base by appealing to "an anxious but powerful dominant caste electorate" (Wilkerson, 2020, p. 326).

Along these lines, the threat is understood as greatest for the *least well off* and *most precariously situated* members of the dominant caste—in particular, the less socioeconomically successful and educated individuals at the bottom of the white hierarchy (Hoffman, 2021; Wilkerson, 2020). The dominant caste at the top of the hierarchy in the US has long remained Protestant white people of Nordic, Anglo-Saxon, and other Northern European origins, particularly those whose families have been in this country for several generations—and threat arises when those designated as "bottom dwellers," particularly black Americans, do not remain in their "designated place" (Wilkerson, 2020, p. 269).

Here let me introject that it is useful to understand that the notion of *caste*, a social construct and an organizing principle of structural racism, runs much deeper than both *race* (in which skin color is an attribute) and *class*; moreover, though caste is only one of several key variables contributing to prevailing cultural anxieties, "[N]o aspect of American life can be fully understood without considering *caste* and *embedded hierarchy*" (ibid., p. 324, italics added). In contrast to racial categorizations and divisions by skin color, rankings in a caste system reflect the human impulse to create hierarchies that goes back millennia, across cultures and societies.

It is noteworthy that sociologists studying hierarchical societal rankings observe a ubiquitous yearning for proximity to the dominant caste that is inherent to any caste system—be it, for example, in India, Nazi Germany, or the United States (ibid.). As I noted in footnote 2 of Chapter 2, because being white and of dominant status is especially seductive for lower-caste whites and even non-whites and recent immigrants, many will vote against their own interests in order to strengthen their proximity to the dominant, white caste.

How might we better understand the confluence of factors accounting for the rise of such destructive thinking and malignancy of psychotic proportions in the American political body, as well as the fact that this comes as a shocking surprise to a large swath of the population? Here again, psychoanalytic insights offer greater clarity.

A psychoanalytic understanding of the psychotic, delusional mode within the group mind

Psychoanalysis has long been concerned with the psychotic element in the psyche and the ways in which psychotic and perverse thinking oscillate with the non-psychotic, healthier parts of the mind, both in individuals and in the group mind of social systems. These dimensions in larger groups have been addressed in ways that help illuminate the extreme thinking characterizing Trumpism, actively manifest over the course of Trump's four years in office and beyond. Several psychoanalytic strands, initially evident in Freud's (1921) ideas on mass psychology and Bion's (1961) observations of regressive group functioning, are particularly useful in unmasking the unconsciously malignant processes in large-group movements. Consequently, the seminal understandings of José Bleger, Elliott Jaques, Erich Fromm, Otto Kernberg, Herbert Rosenfeld, Vamık Volkan, Christopher Bollas, and other analysts interested in group relations aid us in examining the role played by delusional, psychotic structures in both the individual psyche and in social institutions and movements.

It is important to note, however, that such large groups as social and political institutions serve many important functions for their members, including opportunities through social cooperation and constructive activities for expressing and gratifying libidinal impulses, as well as occasions for creative sublimation. Equally significant, however, groups bind members together to defend against unconscious, more primitive anxieties, and to do so requires a healthy *containing frame* or *second skin*. Because of the latter function, groups tend to be particularly resistant to social change inasmuch as change threatens to disturb the group's existing defenses against unconscious psychotic anxieties that are protected by the framing container or skin. Arguably, then, as this book's theme elucidates, in order to understand and possibly alter large-group functioning, it is necessary to go beyond the manifest, conscious, or preconscious level to address the unconscious defenses and underlying fantasy formations that tend to be avoided, often by virulent forms of resistance.

Elliott Jaques (1955) applied Kleinian thinking, along with Freud's and Bion's insights, to address institutional structures in large groups, arguing that many social phenomena show a strikingly close correspondence with psychotic processes in individuals. Using his own experiences in group work to inform his studies, he described how institutions are used by their members to reinforce individual defenses against anxiety, and in particular against a recurrence of the earliest paranoid and depressive anxieties.[2]

Several years later, José Bleger (1967), in discussing Jaques's (1955) work, noted that social institutions serve many functions, one of which is defending against the unconscious psychotic anxieties of individual members. Bleger posited that the institution, much like the *frame* in psychoanalysis, serves as "the depository of the psychotic part of the personality" (1967, p. 514), and by implication, the institutional frame's stability—analogous to the analytic frame—unconsciously provides the illusion of a secure symbiosis that capably holds and contains psychotic anxieties. However, when the institutional frame fails, the psychotic anxieties emerge and become evident in paranoia and violent insurrectionist elements. In the body politic, then, violent emotions often predominate, and the psychotic portion of the group's mind takes hold. From a Bionian group perspective (Bion, 1961), *basic assumptions* take hold under such circumstances and *group-think* is more akin to *group-non-think*.

To be sure, the psychotic mind operating in malignant groups easily becomes susceptible to conspiratorial thinking and malevolent leadership by demagogues and autocrats. Like the *psychotic part of the mind* that Bion (1957) described, it is a mode of thinking that *turns away from reality* when terrifying and turbulent emotions are activated—such as when existential, annihilating, and persecutory fears are triggered. An example of this is the dread evoked by the "Great Replacement" in which "undeserving" groups are viewed as somehow surpassing the more established and traditionally dominant mainstream. In malignant larger

---

[2] It is noteworthy that Jaques, presaging Herbert Rosenfeld's (1984, 1987) contribution, sought to consider how the mechanisms of projective and introjective identification operate in linking individual and social behavior.

groups, thinking shuts down when the psychotic part of the group mind is unable to find a home in a sufficiently *containing object*. Lacking a healthy institutional frame (and a benign leader), dynamic and intolerably complex realities tend to be rendered static, and a delusional sense of control may be created through omnipotent processes (Bergstein, 2020; Kernberg, 2020; see also Rosenfeld, 1984, 1987). In short, when the group ego detaches from that aspect of external reality that is unbearably threatening, an alternative, *delusional fantasy reality* is established in its place (Freud, 1924a). In order to maintain the conviction that the delusional fantasy, such as a conspiratorial belief, is the only reality, perceptions and collusive ideas are sought (Freud, 1924b). For instance, to support the belief that liberal Democrats belong to a satanic pedophilic cult, corroborating "evidence" is proffered on media sites, often through digitally falsified photographs.

Meanwhile, the *non-psychotic*, healthier part of the mind, be it in an individual or in the group's collective mind, proceeds to operate more normally, and thus in its commonplace appearance may confuse or even delude the observer. Not infrequently, many observers of the group fail to see what might be hiding in plain sight: namely, the retreat from an awareness of reality that has taken over in a political group dominated by binary, conspiratorial thinking; such thinking is marked by moral superiority over an evil, satanic opponent (i.e., *Manichean duality*). Consequently, onlookers outside the group often fail to recognize that a *psychotic mythopoesis* operates, in which a perverse madness manages to suck in so many (Bollas, 2020).

Expanding on these ideas, Herbert Rosenfeld, an eminent Kleinian analyst working with psychotic patients, presented a 1984 lecture to the German Psychoanalytic Association (DPV) in which he drew attention to the commonality between the *narcissistic psychotic delusional structure* in patients and the dictatorial state—"political organizations that often dominate an entire state" (Rosenfeld, 1984, p. 78), as reflected in Germany's Third Reich.[3]

[3] Rosenfeld's 1984 lecture "Narcissism and Aggression," presented at the DPV Congress on November 23, 1984, was published the following year and translated from the German by Helen Schoenhals Hart (cited on the American Psychoanalytic Association's Listserv on November 21, 2020).

Rosenfeld argues that in destructive narcissism—whether within the individual psyche or in the regressed group—the *existence of a leader* or *Führer* is absolutely essential. This seductive, charismatic leader is omnipotent (though at first glance not especially sadistic), admired for his power, is typically described as *hypnotic*, and makes exciting, persuasive, and propaganda-laced speeches. Such oral rhetoric lures additional, healthy parts of the person or group into a psychotic world that promises an absence of pain, while enabling and even encouraging the free and complete expression of sadistic tendencies. Though Rosenfeld wrote in the era of totalitarian leaders such as Hitler and Stalin, long before Trump's emergence on the political scene, we might ponder the omnipotence and sadism inherent in the seemingly innocuous slogan "Make America great again!"

Setting out from his understanding of the psychotically delusional patient, Rosenfeld notes that there is a deep sense of inferiority and a murderous envy of everyone whose ability and success appear superior and out of reach; moreover, the leader in this psychotic intrapsychic world is sadistic, omnipotent, and completely non-empathic. This internal *Führer* requires absolute obedience from all parts of the self, and for those parts (or individual members) who show even the least resistance, there is danger of being killed. However, this unbearable situation is secretly converted into one that gives the individual—including the individual-within-the-group—a strong, megalomaniac sense of self, bolstered by hearing the leader/director's threatening voice demanding that destructive/self-destructive acts be committed in order to prove loyalty to the group and leader.

Expanding on Rosenfeld's view, Kernberg (1992) observed that such aggressively perverse object relations entail the defensive utilization of early omnipotent fantasies that originally emerged out of intense frustration, trauma, and pain. When an individual or group is functioning under these conditions, the control of the object becomes central, and intense hatred, paranoia, and sadism go hand in hand. In his discerning analysis suggestive of how a personality cult might be established, Rosenfeld theorizes that when groups regress to this psychotic level, instead of a hypnotically regressed individual entering a trance, millions of people become susceptible to mesmerization by the omnipotent leader's propaganda that promises dominance over the *other* (e.g., liberal elites and invading minorities; Jews in Nazi Germany). Consequently, much like the leader of an individual mind's psychotic organization, the group's *Führer-like leader* gives permission to sadistically attack and rob the demonized other—identified as a dangerous enemy of the community—and even to exterminate them. Implicitly or explicitly, the leader's sadistic supporters are praised for these transgressions.

When such a group's leader functions as a demagogue, using his charisma to lie and foment terrifying anxieties, something akin to a satanic religion or cult typically arises in individual minds within the regressed group (Lifton, 2020). Particularly within the "true believer's" mind, then, satanic objects compete with good objects, and the inverted, paranoid state of mind is one in which those who are experienced as *not with me* are believed to be *against me* in a life-and-death, Manichean battle for survival.

At the center of a psychotic omnipotent system, such as the one that dominated the German nation during parts of the twentieth century and one that has recently threatened the US, is the dangerous twisting and distorting of facts and reality. Moreover, such twists and distortions seem somehow justified in the service of an omnipotent ideal (to "make America great again"). In discussing what happened in mid-twentieth-century Germany, Rosenfeld stated that such a tragic distortion of reality seems identical to the *envious distortion* seen in the delusional patient who feels persecuted by and wishes to harm exactly those people whom he used to admire, even idealize.

In short, Rosenfeld posits many similarities between a psychotic individual and a nation run by an authoritarian dictator such as Hitler—or perhaps by a "wannabe" autocrat (albeit ultimately an unsuccessful one) who operates as a pre-fascist agitator, as Trump has. In Rosenfeld's paradigm, gang fantasies increase the power of omnipotent, destructive narcissism; consider, for example, Nazi gangs, Antifa, or satanic Democratic Party child pornography rings. Even organized crime rings (such as the "Mafia") or their counterparts often loom large in the delusional worlds of patients, as well as of psychotically regressed groups.

Such pathological mental organizations resemble fascist states of mind that tend to be rigidly unyielding in their narcissistic, perverse, and psychotic features (Loewenstein, 2017, 2020). For example, large-group perversity is evident among those Trumpists who idealize "strength" fueled by hatred—for example, of immigrants, non-whites, and elites—and who view love—for example, the more benevolent, socially liberal acceptance of such others—as "weak and contemptible" (Moss, 2021, p. 359). Based on his examination of the Third Reich, Rosenfeld felt that when a psychotic, omnipotent structure *overwhelms an entire nation*, the subsequent road to recovery is very difficult. Given that Trump's tenure as president has ended, there is hope, as I will contend in Chapter 6, that this may not be so in the US—at least for now.

Next, I will explore how we might better understand how psychotic processes develop, function, and are maintained in regressive groups, both among Trump supporters and among anti-Trumpists.

How large-group regression produces cultism

Now let's try to understand more fully how psychotic malignancies have flourished among so many to create a cult-like following within the radically populist movement of Trumpism, along with the role played by Trump as the group's leader. The eminent psychoanalytically oriented psychiatrist and psychohistorian Robert Jay Lifton (2020) has written extensively about how large groups become cultist as well as totalitarian (and function more psychotically). In considering the contemporary US, Lifton posits that there are two main factors accounting for the cultist nature of Trumpism: first, the need for an omnipotent guide in response to human frailty and helplessness, often facilitated by trauma and conditions of heightened fear and anxiety; and second, a vision or illusion of overcoming death (and time), usually influenced by the apocalyptic twins of nuclear and climate-change threats and augmented by today's COVID-19 crisis.

Lifton, like Rosenfeld, posits that, often by means of something akin to a *hypnotic trance state* (en masse), the cultist group promises revitalization, rebirth, or spiritual transcendence. For instance, in interviewing Albert Speer, the former Nazi minister and close ally of Adolf Hitler, Lifton ascertained that Speer frequently found himself in a "dream-like state" and was "drunk" on Hitler's words. This seems quite similar to what happens at Trump's MAGA rallies, in which slogans such as "Make America great again!" or "Lock her up!"—and at the January 6, 2021 insurrection in which an agitated and pugnacious mob chanted

"Stop the steal" and "Hang Mike Pence"—come to serve as mantra-like, hypnotic suggestions that evoke rapturous group fantasies.

Much as Fromm (1955) and later both Volkan (2020) and Kernberg (2020) address, even more benign followers of the cult's leader (e.g., Hitler, Trump) operate within what Lifton terms *malignant normality*. The power of such group internalization is often underestimated, partly due to what Hannah Arendt (1963) termed the *banality of evil* that arises from a failure to think. This conceptualization is related to what Martha Nussbaum (2018) sees as the impact of excessive fear on the capacity to empathize. In cults in which destructive populism has fully taken hold, followers are socialized to negatively and positively hallucinate, attack reason and reality, project judgment and faith into the leader, and engage in actions that support the leader's narcissistic and paranoid view (which at the extreme may lead to destroying or killing any opposition to the cultist ideology).

In the following chapter, I will consider how a malignant leader such as Trump, much like other *prophets of deceit* (Löwenthal & Guterman, 1949), gains power through agitating, persuasive, and perverted tactics that exacerbate rather than transform social distress and existential angst. Consequently, such tactics and techniques encourage a susceptible, regressed group toward processes of identification that increase the demagogue's control. Before doing so, however, in this chapter's final section, I will examine the operation of psychotic group processes that are *not* restricted solely to the large, regressed faction comprising the cult of Trumpism—instead often functioning more insidiously among liberal-thinking groups.

Regressive group processes among anti-Trumpists

It is important to recognize that such regressive processes are *not* restricted to those on the right of the political spectrum. Chrzanowski (2019), unlike most liberal thinkers, skillfully adumbrates how Trump's detractors often fall into a regressive, manic group process that is "organized around primitive unanimity and anonymity that developed into … *basic assumption phenomena*" (p. 717), particularly that of *fight-flight* (e.g., angry negation) and *pairing* (i.e., excited agreement). In essence, Trump's crude provocations can serve to increase psychotic anxieties among his challengers, who become less capable of symbolic thinking on their own. Consequently, Trump detractors have been liable to fall into fantasy-based thought in which the omnipotent force of common hatred would make Trump (and Trumpism) simply disappear, particularly if truth (and reality) were to be revealed.

By dint of the "strict denial of psychotic instability in group experience" (p. 724)—much as Bollas (2018, 2020) suggests—a delusional vulnerability and a dissociative tendency arise among Trump detractors, just as among Trump supporters, which can lead to a guileless expectation for "the goodness of the 'supposed group' to prevail" (p. 718). This can result in a form of *demophobia* in which the "common" masses become demonized (Müller, 2021).

Continuing along Kleinian and Bionian lines, we note that with the assumption of a holistic, cohesive, orderly, and rational whole-object rather than a part-object, there is a tendency to assume that the mother's body will survive or be unaffected by a psychotic, unstructured part-object environment. Consequently, many on the left, operating from liberal, Enlightenment thinking, fall into the naïve illusion that every group is or must be "an orderly, rational 'place'" (Chrzanowski, 2019, p. 718). This disconnect has led to an inordinate focus on Trump's personality and mendacity; moreover, his detractors reductively and one-dimensionally tend to expect that all Trump supporters think similarly regarding his character.

This aspect of leftist psychotic thinking can take the form of a *negative hallucination* that disavows or leaves unrecognized Trump's populism as representative of the total (national) group situation's reality. Thus, many detractors fail to understand why attacks on Trump's flawed personality (especially his mendacity, corruption, and destructiveness) have been unsuccessful in undermining his popularity and power (ibid.). Instead, by inordinately focusing on his personality and fallaciously assuming that his supporters will come to similar conclusions about his character, anti-Trumpists have found that such attacks serve only to increase his popularity in the destructive populist dynamic (Zienert-Eilts, 2020).

CHAPTER 5

The malignant leader's "perversion" of the containing function and the perils of cultism

> *The techniques of the demagogue and the hypnotist coincide … by which individuals are made to undergo the regressions which reduce them to mere members of a group.*
>
> —Theodor Adorno (1951, p. 123)

Karin Johanna Zienert-Eilts (2020) developed the useful concept of *perverted containing*, applying it to her understanding of the destructive populist social movement known as Trumpism. Building from Bion's notion of the primordial terror of being ejected from the motherly container, she argued that within large-group social processes, unconscious archaic fears of life-threatening annihilation and envious hatred are released through a social erosion process; these fears serve as the linchpin for destructive forms of populism. Consequently, *fragmentation (splitting)* takes place both within individuals and between social groups/populations—for instance, between rich and poor, elites and commoners, natives and immigrants, whites and non-whites—and thus, *sufficient containment* by the ruling parties (and structures) becomes essential for necessary reassurance and stability.

In accordance with Jaques's (1955) and Bleger's (1967) ideas about the social institutional frame's holding function, healthy containment entails an elastic organ or institutional object operating with a detoxifying, metabolizing, and transforming function (of potentially destructive processes): namely, an *alpha-functioning* object (Bion, 1962). In contrast to *basic assumption* group functioning (Bion, 1961), the specialized work group functions to *neutralize*—that is, to contain psychotic anxieties (Bion, 1962)—and the work group leader's virtuous qualities serve as an *ego ideal* (Freud, 1921).

Within the body politic of a sufficiently functioning representative democracy, then, members of the aristocracy of a liberal democracy—experts, government officials, journalists, upstanding politicians and members of the judiciary, educators, elites, and other highly idealized public figures (e.g., public intellectuals, celebrities, athletes, etc.)—who serve the healthy containing function, neutralize the group's psychotic anxieties and fantasies (Chrzanowski, 2019). Political theorists focus on the essential need to structure democracy's inherent tensions stemming from its requirement of successfully functioning *intermediary institutions*, especially within political parties, the judiciary, and the media (Müller, 2021). In this respect, the *sane* components of the collective are not overrun by the *mad* elements. Traditionally in the US, democratically elected leaders and the structures of democracy (e.g., the Constitution, free press, consensual and verifiable truths) tend to serve as sufficient containers in both *motherly* (i.e., alpha functioning) and *fatherly* (i.e., triangular structures that foster symbolization) countenance.

Trumpism as a personality cult

Lifton (2020) elaborated on the operation of cultist *claims to own reality* (i.e., to have sole moral representation). He studied such operations in the form of ideological totalism, in which idea structures claim absolute truth and virtue while seeking to provide meanings and approaches to almost every aspect of life—in, for example, Nazi Germany, Communist China (thought reforms), the Japanese religious cult of Aum Shinrikyo, Donald Trump's approach to reality, etc. The capacity to submit to authoritarian totalism is rooted in the dependencies of childhood and resides in all of us; consequently, cult leaders tend to style themselves along the lines of paternal or maternal figures, protecting their family of followers.

Lifton then identified four ubiquitous themes in such cult-based group forms of totalism, which are apparent in Trump's personality cult. First, there is *milieu control* through the manipulation of communication in the environment. Second, *doctrine over person* means that any doubts a member may have about orthodoxy—including prevailing conspiracy theories, such as QAnon's—are attributed exclusively to the member's personal limitations or individual pathology (and the outlier is often banished).

Next, there is *loading the language*, in which complex problems are condensed into reductionistic, definitive-sounding phrases—and as Bollas (2020) notes, signs come to replace signifiers (e.g., *liberal* or *elite* is equated to evil, *political correctness* becomes an attack on freedom, and *protests* are described as anarchy). Moreover, like the Orwellian concept of *Newspeak*, language is thus turned into a totalitarian, propagandist tool with which to combat complex, critical reasoning—a tool that perverts the relationship between truth and fiction as well as between good and evil. And finally, the *dispensing of existence* results when representatives of the cultist group (e.g., the Michigan militia, Proud Boys, Oath Keepers, Boogaloo Bois, Three Percenters, and arguably perhaps even Antifa) are empowered to decide who has the right to participate—or even to exist.

The drudgery of dealing with reality is abandoned as the group/cult enters a paranoid and psychotic mode of thinking (Hofstadter, 1965; H. Rosenfeld, 1984, 1987) and begins to "bathe in the delights of fantasy" (Bollas, 2020). Like most cultist leaders who are themselves drawn to authoritarian and totalitarian leaders, Trump employs a methodology and set of tactics that reflect the use of hypnotic-like techniques, as well as effectively persuasive salesmanship and branding, in order to establish himself as leader of a destructive populist group process.

Trump's arsenal of methods that serve to impair reality testing and inhibit the capacity to think include: *primitive, brutal rhetoric* and *bullying*; utilizing a *vocabulary of extremes*—for example, "great," "completely," "total," "smartest," "dumbest," etc.; *inflaming his audience's feelings* of exclusion, terror, and rage; maximal *exaggeration of fantasized threats* to his followers (e.g., an apocalyptic future looms that only he can prevent); *dehumanizing his enemies*, whom he regards as undeserving of compassion or feelings of guilt; employment of *constant repetition* (typically of short, two- or three-word phrases); establishment of himself as *the sole protector and solver* of complex problems (e.g., only he can accomplish …: "I alone can fix it"); *bizarre, provocative, omnipotent directives* (e.g., that people should swallow bleach to cure themselves of COVID); engagement in deliberate *breaches of taboos* to authorize destructiveness and psychic incest; actively creating confusions that produce a *perversion of morality* in which corrupt officials become victims, losers become winners, and heroes become suckers; relying on repetitive use of *preferred communication modes* emphasizing speed of dissemination, telegraphic style, superficial appeal, and hyperbolic content (social media modes, such as Twitter, Facebook, etc.); and finally, creation of opportunities to remain in the limelight (either positively or negatively) in *a persistent seeking of attention.*

As a consequence of these ways of operating, cult members end up participating in a form of mass hypnosis in which an altered, hypnotic state supersedes reality testing and critical thinking. As a description of the hypnotic features used to supersede reality testing, the frequently used term *mass hypnosis* is far from precise in portraying a highly complex phenomenon. Nonetheless, the useful concept of *trance logic* is helpful in capturing a state of mind to which many Trump followers fall prey (Orne, 1959). Such "logic" belongs to an altered mental state or trance-like consciousness marked by suspension of the normal capacity for critical analysis and a far greater tolerance for logical inconsistencies, thus opening the individual or group to suggestion. Consequently, when an individual is in a hypnotic trance state, there is greater likelihood that he or she will become ego-syntonically absorbed in a dissociative experience operating outside consensual reality.

For instance, when it is suggested to a deeply hypnotized subject that she or he "sees a pink elephant sitting on a chair," the subject is likely to confirm seeing and even walking around the pink elephant, yet note that the elephant, though appearing very real, seems transparent; thus, the suggested elephant is quite different from other elephants. For his most ardent followers, Trump's deceptions and outright lies become "alternate truths" that often function similarly to "pink elephants," given that his followers—like hypnotized subjects who become archaically involved with (i.e., extremely regressed vis-à-vis) their hypnotist—seem to have fallen under the spell of his charismatic presence.

Trump's autocratic, cult-creating methods

Trump's skill in both fomenting *divisiveness* (populists versus elites) and *attacking democratic ideals and standards* is multi-determined, though it can partially be attributed to his strategy of inspiring loyalty by fanning the flames of fear and offering a safe space of shamelessness in which his supporters cannot be judged in moral terms. In this context, his detractors (liberal elites, Democrats, leftists, socialists, critics from "fake news" sites, and politically correct zealots, as well as academics and scientists) come across as sanctimoniously judgmental of his "regular," salt-of-the-earth followers. As a man of the "real" (not "fake") people, Trump, and Trump only, then, serves as the charismatic and protective strongman—very much as a *caudillo*, a democratically elected, autocratic populist who exercises power as a political leader in authoritarian ways that are subject neither to shame nor to comparison with norms.

By creating chaos and fomenting divisiveness that promotes greater uncertainty, Trump instills in his followers the feeling of having less control over their circumstances. Thus, they experience greater vulnerability and are more likely to entrust their fate to a higher power or would-be "messiah" (cf. Bion, 1961; Hoffman, 2018). In quite a treacherous and perverse irony, only he can protect his following—meaning, "he alone can fix it"—from the terrifying fears he has provoked (Nussbaum, 2018). Trump both admires and attempts to rule in the tradition of contemporary autocrats and dictators such as Bolsonaro, Erdoğan, Duterte, Orbán, Putin, Lukashenko, Xi Jinping, and Kim Jong-un; consequently, despite lacking any prevailing ideology, he is likely to be viewed historically as functioning in a way akin to that of Pinochet, Franco, Castro, Hugo Chavez, Julius Caesar, and other autocrats who have ruled through their personality (e.g., the Fuhrer, Il Duce, etc.).

As I noted in discussing the perverted containing function of malignant leadership, Trump has all the characteristics of a *destructive populist*; specifically, he is anti-liberal, anti-pluralist, anti-elitist, divisive in terms of good/evil as well as truth/lying, the claimant of sole moral representation, a denier of reality (negative hallucination), one who idealizes narcissistic omnipotence and brutal aggression and who appears to be entirely lacking in any sense of guilt, responsibility, or compassion. In addressing the atrocity of today's pre-fascist, post-truth era, historian Timothy Snyder (2021) regards Trump as the "high priest of the big lie" who has become America's first "post-truth president" through presenting himself as the single source of truth.

Like most demagogues who are adept in the use of agitation despite lacking a consistent ideology, what Trump has in common with other ideological autocrats is the *claim to own reality*. As Kernberg (2020) elaborates, this claim is formed from Trump's psychic processes, which reveal a *solipsistic, narcissistic, and paranoid approach to reality* (in which he bears no responsibility for the larger reality experienced by others or for general standards of evidence of what may be considered "real"). Forensic psychiatrist Bandy X. Lee (2020) pulls no punches in challenging the American Psychiatric Association's controversial "Goldwater Rule" to warn of the serious dangers posed by Trump's *sociopathy* and *pathological narcissism*. It is observable to most that, enclosed within his own bubble, Trump perceives reality with an "anything goes" approach to reporting the truth (Bollas, 2020). As a highly skilled, twenty-first-century *prophet of deceit* (Löwenthal & Guterman, 1949), Trump agitates through hints, allusions, and doubletalk. That is, instead of simply making a statement, "he always hints" (p. 158) at something, while the force he brings to bear (which colludes with his followers' worst instincts) is gained through "thrilling, salacious, or sadistic detail" (p. xxiv).

In distinct contrast, then, to psychoanalysis, which aims to make the unconscious more conscious, a "psychoanalysis in reverse" accrues in which social control is used to expropriate the unconscious through manipulative tactics that serve to promote a state of *non-critical thinking* (Adorno, 1951, p. 118), as well as *non-empathic relating* (Nussbaum, 2018). Italian novelist and philosopher Umberto Eco (1995) suggests that such tactics depend on cult-like *action for action's sake*, conceived with the goal of denying difference and transforming thinking into a form of emasculation. He uses the term *ur-fascism*, or eternal fascism, to describe the inherent fascist principles underlying such tactics.[1]

[1] As noted in Chapter 3 (footnote 2), Trump, despite using fascist tactics, is a demagogue undeserving of the term *fascist* inasmuch as he lacks an ideological purpose.

As H. Rosenfeld (1984, 1987) implies, psychoanalytic understanding and skillful practice can be viewed as an antidote to the seduction of fascist states of mind, both within the individual and, hopefully, among the larger, regressed group drawn into such perverse and psychotic realms of anti-critical thinking.

Austrian psychoanalyst Elisabeth Skale (2021) contends that Trump and other far-right populists skillfully employ social media and computer screens to weaken conceptual thinking as the basis of action by producing "echo chambers." These filtered bubbles resemble Donald Meltzer's (1992) "maternal rectum" in which a *claustrum* emerges that is "dominated by an atmosphere of terror, exposure to sadism, and nameless fear of being 'thrown away'" (Skale, 2021, p. 241). Such techniques used by authoritarian demagogues and neo-fascist leaders serve to keep the most ardent followers "in permanent psychic bondage, to increase and reinforce neurotic and even psychotic behavior culminating in perpetual dependency" (Löwenthal & Guterman, 1949, p. xxiv). Era Loewenstein (2020), a San Francisco-based psychoanalyst, maintains that Trump's fascist technique of agitation aimed at destroying knowledge—in Bionian terms, by creating false links or -*K*—falsifies and obliterates reality rather than providing opportunities to learn from experience.

With this in mind, how might we better understand the rotten or perverse fit that exists between the regressed large group and a leader like Trump?

The rise of perverted containment and a rotten second skin

The *perverse* part of the psyche stands closer to the psychotic realm and is motivated by omnipotence, envy, and hatred. Perversity involves efforts to destroy reality largely through obliterating differences and establishing a new reality; the perverted person becomes excited by contempt for the Law of the Father (Chasseguet-Smirgel, 1984). Viewing Trump through the lens of his perverse character, Loewenstein (2018) argues that in attacking libidinal ties between objects, Trump seeks to "debase the very idea of the president as ... [the nation's] symbolic father or mother ... who abides by the Law" (p. 43). In corrupting the symbolic or paternal function, an idealized "fecal universe" (to employ an especially evocative metaphor, much like Meltzer's *maternal rectum*) is created in which obstacles, boundaries, and differences are eliminated, the aesthetics of beauty and ugliness are altered, and trust and dependence on good objects are attacked (Loewenstein, 2017). In short, there is a tendency to turn the physical environment into a fecal or decomposing, grayish-brown substance in which everything becomes shit except the group and its leader (Dirham, personal communication).

Nonetheless, as I've noted, in drawing on Freud's (1921) and Bion's (1961) understandings, along with observations by analysts who have examined regressed behaviors in large groups (Kernberg, 2020; Turquet, 1975; Volkan, 2004), we can conclude that it is in the nature of large regressed groups to search for leaders who exhibit the syndrome of *malignant narcissism*. Furthermore, employing the *skin-ego* concept, Kernberg (2020) joined with Volkan (2004) to suggest that regressed groups are characterized by the need to locate a *second skin* in order to reestablish the diminished sense of existential security for the group's individual members that traumatic conditions largely obliterate. To reiterate, this leader is sought out by the group to reassure its members in the context of a loss of individualized status and role-based identity (Kernberg, 2020). Once such a leader is found and identified with, group members are provided with the second skin of an idealized mutual identity. A reciprocal, albeit unruly fit occurs between large-group regression and the leader's pathology due to the group's need for a malignantly narcissistic leader characterized by the mutual identification with narcissism, grandiosity, and paranoid trends (ibid.). In short, what I regard as the group's *rotten second skin*, or as I will discuss next, its *perverted containment*, is the result.

In relation to the larger group, *perverted, unhealthy containment* becomes more likely under conditions of regression. Rather than containing by detoxifying and transforming the mad, psychotic elements within the larger group, this brand of containment fuels destructive processes.[2] When attunement by the leader (and accompanying institutional structures) is sufficiently lacking, primitive and weakly symbolized affects (*beta* products, in Bionian language) escalate, and the group

[2] When a leader such as Trump operates as a *perverse container*, he also serves to abolish differences and limit the individuality of group members (Chrzanowski, 2019).

is left bereft of a containing *establishment mother* (Zienert-Eilts, 2020, p. 979) who can metabolize primitive, often unsymbolized (beta) affects.

Moreover, lacking an alpha function—*maternal containment*—with which to address escalating, nameless, archaic fears and under the sway of its mad elements, the group remains characterized by the absence of a sorely needed third in the form of a *symbolizing, paternal function*—a sufficient *establishment father*—who is able to triangulate by facilitating symbolic functioning and thus attenuate the perverted containment. In this way, a healthy containing function can also be established. However, by perversely degrading the law that signifies the symbolizing function through indifference to truth and disdain for facts, a regressive spiral (Kernberg, 2020) is generated, one marked by polarization.

In brief, using Kleinian terms, the normal interplay between paranoid/ schizoid (P/S) and depressive (D) positions becomes more unbalanced and rapidly turns toward the former in such regressive environments. Consequently, when P/S processes—the collective psyche's *mad, psychotic* elements—are fueled rather than contained, beta elements (archaic, negative affects) proliferate in destructive fashion, and the group's dynamics often take on an ecstatic and manic character. We see this, for example, at MAGA rallies, as well as in the violent insurrection of January 6 at the Capitol. By creating an urgent, apocalyptic illusion requiring immediate action, Trump, operating as a rotten, perverted container using skillful oratory, is able to instigate a mob bent on violent actions that lack a rational political aim (Adorno, 1951). As a *prophet of deceit* (Löwenthal & Guterman, 1949) appealing to the group's most primitive, unconscious fears, Trump agitates by identifying the so-called enemy who has been created by splitting off and projecting his most hated parts—an enemy whom the mob is then mobilized to eradicate (Loewenstein, 2018).

Trump as the perverted container and rotten second skin in a destructive populist fit

Trump as *the perverted container* appears in the same paranoid/schizoid mode as the larger group—speaking the same language and sharing "the hatred of the 'establishment mother'" (Zienert-Eilts, 2020, p. 980). Hence a *destructive populist fit* is formed and tends to quickly become sealed; this skin that holds the group together by means of a reassuring mutual identification is fundamentally a *rotten skin*. Living in a "post-truth" bubble that has fomented a historical crisis in which verifiable truth is repeatedly hijacked by misinformation, Trump stands as "both a *symptom* and an *acceleration* of our move away from shared standards of truth" (S. Rosenfeld, 2019, p. 5, italics added).

Indeed, today we live in what can be justifiably called a *post-truth era,* and lies, particularly what are frequently referred to as *big lies*—for instance, that the 2020 presidential election was "stolen"—are rampant. *The Washington Post* recently reported that over the course of Trump's four years in office, he made more than 30,000 false and misleading claims. Historian Timothy Snyder (2017) pointed out that attacks on truth—in which opinions and emotional rhetoric take precedence over consensual reality, provable facts, and empirical truths—have historically been a precursor to fascism, enabling charismatic politicians and demagogues to step in and fill the vacuum where truth once was.

The regressed large group's delusional, conspiratorial ideas have found their match in Trump's attacks on reality and in his paranoid thinking, thereby creating a *folie à deux* in which delusional and persecutory ideas are shared by those forming a social unit. Kernberg (2020) terms this a *malignant normalcy*, whereas Löwenthal and Guterman (1949) referred to a *lunatic fringe* coopting the mainstream, and Fromm (1955), in discussing sick societies, declared that "just as there is a *folie à deux,* there is a *folie à millions*" (p. 14).

In destructive-populist group organization dynamics, a charismatic leader operating as a messiah in accordance with basic assumption mentality fulfills the group's narcissistically omnipotent desires by promising to defeat and destroy all (projected) evil. When fears of increasing anarchy and potential apocalyptic disaster are repeatedly stoked, complex reality is simplified and manically distorted through exaggeration of threatening and aggressive content.

For instance, consider Trump's earlier false claims pertaining to Obama's foreign birth, and his later statements that US borders were becoming overrun by criminals, rapists, and terrorists—problems that only Trump's border wall would resolve. These extreme falsehoods would subsequently morph into conspiratorial appeals focused on witch hunts, "Russian hoaxes," "Pizzagate" and QAnon, Antifa, the Black Lives Matter movement, socialism and Hugo Chavez, and the "stolen" election. Moreover, according to Trump's branding, he alone is the "stable genius" who can "fix" the country by serving as its secular savior. Contributing to this is his construction of a great wall to offer the messianic promise of complete and permanent safety.

Despite Trump's loss of the 2020 election, the cult of Trumpism continues to flourish and to trade in conspiratorial delusions. Even when a cherished belief is clearly contradicted by verifiable evidence—such as that the election was "stolen"—many cult members remain strongly attached to that belief and its promise of a return to earlier, idealized times. Social psychology supplements psychoanalytic thinking by positing the theory of *cognitive dissonance* to explain what happens when prophecies fail and yet the delusional belief is maintained, especially when there is group support for the fantasy (Festinger, 1957; Festinger et al., 1956). We see this among many Trumpists who follow QAnon and remain convinced that a storm is coming to sweep away a cabal of Satan-worshipping, pedophilic Democrats and restore Trump as the country's rightfully elected leader.

Zienert-Eilts (2020) suggests that "the connection between a destructive populist leader and his followers is so closely merged … that the destructive dynamics do not find reassurance, but on the contrary need to be constantly fueled" (p. 978). As boundaries are dissolved, reality-based ego functions are reduced, sadistic aspirations are satisfied, destructiveness is idealized, and good and evil—as well as truth and lying—are perverted. Group members' individual identities—characterized by powerlessness, humiliation, and helplessness—are typically replaced by a destructive group identity that serves to *confirm* rather than *transform* destructive elements. This has been described as a "double omnipotent destructive group identity" (Zienert-Eilts, 2020, p. 980), which entails: (1) a symbiotic identification with the destructive paranoid/schizoid (P/S) leader—namely, Trump; and (2) an identification with other group members in a similar P/S mode. This is another way in which the second skin provided by Trump (and Trumpism) is *rotten*, particularly in its virulent and perverse destructiveness.

However, not all followers of Trump fall into the camp of fanatics who stick with the perverted container in the paranoid–schizoid (P/S) mode; others become disappointed or disillusioned and move between the P/S and depressive (D) modes. Still, a great many remain adhesively or symbiotically tied to Trump; in this respect, cultism takes hold and Trumpism manifests as a personality cult. How might we understand how a large group becomes cultist?

Demagoguery, American autocratic trends, and the danger to democracy

Trump uses demagoguery to incite large crowds and manipulate their emotions, particularly fear and rage, priming them not only to act in ways that are against their better interests, but to destroy the very democratically based institutions and standards that exist to protect and serve them. As I have discussed, psychoanalysts consider these standards and institutions in terms of the nation's healthy *container*, *frame*, or *second skin*. As taken up in Chapter 2, American populism and the accompanying autocratic trends have long been fueled by the mythic idea of American *exceptionalism*—a *manifest destiny* in which the darker side of authority and global power is seen as deserving to prevail.[3] During the last half decade, these conditions have been frighteningly ascendant. In sharp contrast to Abraham Lincoln's adage that "right makes might," today the reverse seems true as our morality tends to be perverted. We are forced to acknowledge that, as was graphically displayed at the Capitol on January 6 and subsequently sanctioned by a large faction of the Republican members of Congress—who ideally would have served as the intermediaries necessary for democracy to function successfully—shamelessness is taking the place of righteousness.

The belief in a manly superiority, the remnants of which continue to operate today, has long been regarded as part of America's destiny—an aggression and often an accompanying destructiveness that once characterized the antebellum United States (Shapiro, 2020, p. 53). Moreover, when fascist propaganda renders critical thinking itself a form of emasculation, and action is privileged simply for its own sake (Eco, 1995), a phallic form of masculinity begins to dominate over a shamefully inferior femininity.

[3] *Manifest destiny*, a theme prominent in US history and reflective of the American sense of mission, encompasses both benign and aggressive ideals and actions (Hofstadter, 1965).

As I suggested in describing Trump's *perversion* of the leader's containing function (and the *rottenness* of the needed second skin), in today's imagined "return to greatness," Trump's brazen belligerence, his crassness and shamelessness are perversely seen by his followers as courage and strength. This aberrant, often toxic form of masculinity disdains restraint, thoughtfulness, empathy, and moral bravery; instead, the aggressive and action-driven persona of "real" men is viewed as superior to that of inferior, more "feminine" men who are less likely to advocate war, unrestricted gun ownership, border walls, fast cars, Trump rallies, etc. This more polarized, "dramatic disparagement of femininity … [leads] … to *dramatic distinction between genders*" (Hoffman, 2018, p. 270, italics added).

Consequently, blatantly not caring that others might be horrified, Trump was able to get away with boasting about grabbing women's genitals and repeatedly calling his presidential rival by the pejorative "Sleepy Joe," thereby legitimizing a form of rudeness and bullying that most of us take pains to teach our children not to engage in. Furthermore, Trump insinuated that Biden's age had caused cognitive impairment, discounted John McCain's military service and heroism, insulted the Gold Star Muslim parents of a slain American soldier, physically stalked Hillary Clinton in an intimidating fashion during their presidential debate, and even declared that he could commit murder on New York's Fifth Avenue without fear of reprisal.

As Shakespearian scholar James Shapiro (2020) notes in citing historian Amy Greenberg (2005), Trump's aberrant masculinity demonstrates a long-standing conflict in the competing versions of masculinity evident in the US today. These alternative masculinities are well illustrated in the contrast between the *restrained masculinity* of Barack Obama, viewed as a sensitive, thoughtful, more elite man (much like Abraham Lincoln), and the *martial masculinity* of Donald Trump, who resembles Andrew Jackson in embodying a brash and coarse, perhaps "toxic" form of manhood. The martial version of manhood tends to manifest in extreme ways among male members of "the real people"—the common (white) man—who feel left behind during periods of rapid economic and cultural transformation, plagued by inequities of status and income despite their relatively privileged position as white natives.

At the extremes, *restrained masculinity* embraces moderation, compassion, domesticity, dignity, graciousness, self-reflection, sensitivity, and gentlemanliness, as well as being morally upright, reliable, and courageously engaging in the search for verifiable truth. In contrast, *martial manhood* is unfiltered and ruthless, characterized by greater tolerance for excess, physicality, domination, extreme competitiveness, lack of empathy, a dog-eat-dog worldview, and gallantry in battle. Despite the polarity between restrained and martial masculinities, however, most American men experience a combination of varieties of manhood that lie along a continuum; perhaps this was best represented in the twentieth century by the combined, complex forms of masculinity seen in figures such as Theodore Roosevelt, Ernest Hemingway, Malcolm X, and Muhammad Ali.

Psychoanalysts have discussed these two typically more oscillating types of manhood along Freudian lines, describing the more mature version of manhood as primarily reflecting a *genital masculinity* that integrates phallic propensities while recognizing the subjectivity of others in aiming for greater connection—in contrast to *phallic masculinity*, which is more dominant in childhood and adolescence in its taste for controlling, conquering, and vanquishing (serving both adaptive and maladaptive ends; Diamond, 2021). In a multitude of ways, Trump reflects a very extreme version of phallic or martial masculinity, in which male development is arrested in its childhood and adolescent phases. This is evident in the fact that most of his detractors, and even many of his enablers, see him as essentially an impulsive and petulant man-child in need of adult supervision.

I will next briefly consider that despite Trump's being out of presidential office, Trumpism as a personality cult remains the predominant driver of the Republican party, in which Trump himself retains a profound hold on the nation while representing a serious danger to American democracy.

Trumpism and the potential erosion of democracy

American populism in an authoritarian context is evident in Trump's *neoliberalism* (and the more extreme version, *illiberalism*) in which the individual self is prioritized, particularly as a "strong winner" in contrast to a "vulnerable loser." Hence, there is a heavy emphasis on individual rights ("don't tread on me"), in which, for example, the freedom *not* to wear a mask, not to socially distance or to be vaccinated, takes precedence over the collective good (reducing the spread of illness to others). In the current era of democracy being under siege, it no longer appears to make a great deal of sense to polarize *left* versus *right* or *liberal* versus *conservative*—instead, we hear of *liberal democracy* being pitted against *illiberalism* (or *neoliberalism*).

As I've suggested, psychoanalytic insights are invaluable in order to better understand the currents of contemporary populism and its destructive tenets and psychotic elements. In this book's penultimate chapter, I will make use of our psychoanalytic understanding of these disturbing factors, as well as related understandings, in order to suggest ways to reestablish a sufficiently containing, institutional frame in the body politic. That is, I will present approaches to both attenuate the potency of destructive, psychotic elements and to strengthen the non-pathological elements in the nation as a whole.

CHAPTER 6

Containing Trumpism and destructive populism: addressing, encompassing, and restraining regressive malignant dynamics

When the bough breaks, the cradle will fall. And down will come baby, cradle and all.

—"Rock-a-Bye Baby," eighteenth-century nursery rhyme

Throughout his reign as president and despite losing the 2020 election, Donald Trump's will to expand his power and his malignant narcissism have largely remained uncontained, and were perhaps even strengthened as a result of his being acquitted in a second impeachment trial. Moreover, Trumpism's destructive populism persists in the form of corruption and anti-democratic actions and policies evident in many US institutions, politicians, and undertakings, such as the Republican party's forceful suppression of voting rights, its attempt to curtail the right to peacefully assemble, and its flagrant effort to obstruct an independent, bipartisan congressional investigation of the seditious insurrection at the Capitol on January 6, 2021. In conjunction with the growing extremist insurrectionist movement, prominent educator and journalist Mark Danner (2021), after describing his experience as a participant observer on January 6 and in agreement with most other informed thinkers, foretold that Trump's millions of angry and politicized followers will not disappear, but rather "will remain as a lurking poison … ready to be activated, and [that] their nihilistic rejections of … institutions and laws will only grow more venomous" (p. 8).

Methods for a turbulent nation

Danner's prediction is quite disturbing for most of us; however, the apprehensions and fears that accompany the recognition of imminent threat are not necessarily problematic in that they can function much like *signal anxiety*: an alarm that mobilizes the nation's collective ego, spurring it on to adapt to the dangers posed by external reality and to achieve greater mastery of them. Irish intellectual Fintan O'Toole (2021) aptly writes from abroad in considering the necessity of fear-induced action in order to achieve greater security in the midst of the current worldwide crisis:

> Without an urgent anxiety about the near-death of the American republic, about the pandemic, about the terrors of climate change, about the insupportable nature of racial injustice, about the incompatibility of gross inequality and democracy, there can be no hope. (p. 10)

Not unexpectedly and fortunately, the extent of the militancy in Trump's "army" of disgruntled followers continues to be made known, requiring attention and skillful containment by the "less mad" and "saner" factions of the political body. Consequently, much as we may do when working with an individual patient, we might ask ourselves whether the "mad" or "bad" parts of the polity can be brought more in line with the "sane," healthier elements, resulting in less detrimental functioning and greater collective wholeness. In particular, what can we as psychoanalysts bring to the table during such perilous times?

To repeat what has been stated from the outset, it is crucial to determine how to negotiate reality with Trumpism, or at least to contain its prevailing extremism, rather than maintaining an irreconcilable schism. I've argued that the potential for this rests partially on our recognition of the fundamental uncertainty inherent in democratic societies, which can unleash terrifying existential fears under certain social conditions, especially when fueled by agitating, malignant leadership. However, hopefulness grounded in a reality that encompasses insight into the forces at play—contra paralyzing fears, helplessness, and apathy—can lead to plausibly successful efforts and an activism that addresses the impact of destructive forces operative in malignant group regression.

As I will address further in the book's concluding chapter (Chapter 7), much as in psychoanalytic treatment itself, hope for a valued outcome in the sociopolitical sphere—a kind of hope that fuels agency and practical action, making use of dynamic insights—is necessary for the preservation of democracy in the context of today's rising authoritarianism, massive uncertainty, and virulent attacks on consensual truths. Moreover, if the situation is to improve, we must employ what might be seen as the *essential third* to tolerate and encompass the inevitable tension within US democracy—namely, a dialectic between what I've described in Chapter 2 as *the people* and *the elites* (or, in more economic imagery, between Main Street and Wall Street).

A more nuanced view of the country's competitive tensions in relation to status is suggested by award-winning journalist George Packer (2021b), who argues that four essential divisions within the large group are each characterized by a specific narrative that must coexist despite integral conflicts with the other three. These divisions are: (1) *Free America*, which celebrates the energy of the unencumbered individual; it is informed by libertarianism, individualism, and strands of the conservative movement with its seeds of crony capitalism; (2) *Smart America*, which respects intelligence and welcomes change; it embraces capitalism and the principle of meritocracy that results in a contemporary form of inequality; (3) *Real America* represents a renewed anti-elitism and anti-intellectualism largely among working-class whites, committing itself to a populist nationalism that is threatened by contamination from without and betrayal from within; and (4) *Just America*, which arises in the face of persistent injustice, declining social mobility, and increasing inequality, demanding a confrontation with the country's fixed-caste hierarchy and citing a betrayal by the elites' complacent meritocracy.

It should be noted that these are not factions inescapably seeking to crush one another in a utopian quest to eradicate conflict and resentment. In short, among these (and more generally among similar social divisions), neither complete separateness nor conquest is tenable.

In this chapter, I propose some ideas that might be helpful in recognizing that so much of the ideology in the regressive, destructive, and conspiratorial thinking of Trumpism is largely designed to destroy any possibility of a *shared third* or a constructive, *containing frame* from which to create a stronger foundation for existing together in accordance with the reality principle. Consequently, because political resistance to Trumpism's stance is so incommensurable with its prevailing view of reality, it becomes extremely challenging to find ways to share an ideological or historical reality.

A key issue, then, is how we might create, maintain, and more effectively deal with an ideology—actually, more of an *anti-ideology*, one that is more nihilistically geared toward tearing apart healthier symbolic functioning—and that seems to more ruthlessly and successfully attack any containing frame that otherwise holds the psychotic "mad" part of the collective in check (Bleger, 1967; Jaques, 1955; H. Rosenfeld, 1987). It is noteworthy, however, that in the 1940s and 50s, many leading thinkers within the Frankfurt School (discussed in Chapters 1, 2, and 5) sought to expose the tricks and devices used by authoritarian and fascist leaders (Adorno, 1951; Arato & Gebhardt, 1982; Löwenthal & Guterman, 1949). These scholars hoped that the manipulative, controlling tactics that perpetuate emotional aggravation might be disarmed by "vaccinating" the public through providing cognitive tools (for instance, by distributing pamphlets) that would counter anti-cognitive attacks on critical thinking. Unfortunately, nothing substantive came of this practical, rationalist effort. Still, the Frankfurt School's research data and analytic methods may well prove helpful—in combination with contemporary psychoanalytic insights, especially those pertaining to regressive group functioning—as we develop strategies for addressing the current sociopolitical schism in which competing factions are trapped in separate, impenetrable bubbles.

Nonetheless, gaining mastery over regressive, malignant group dynamics is a monumental challenge that requires numerous and varied approaches. For these approaches to be effective, *humanitarian impulses* must be combined with greater *insight as to the unconscious group dynamics* and concomitant *social leadership* that render individuals susceptible to paranoid, conspiratorial, and destructive forms of populist thinking.

To further a dialogue along these lines that remains cognizant of the inherent unconscious conflicts and tensions in need of a suitable restraining frame, and in utilizing understandings from psychoanalysis as well as psychology and the social sciences, I posit five key dimensions, each of which will address several ambitions as discussed in the subsections to follow.

Employing psychoanalytic understandings of unconscious group dynamics and non-rational thinking

As Hofstadter (1965) implied, the complexity of political action can be understood and altered only through rendering the *non-rational side of politics* more conscious—clearly opening the door for psychoanalysts and the role of the unconscious to enter. More than a half century ago, he made abundantly clear the need to apply a sophisticated, deep psychological understanding—namely, a psychoanalytic perspective—to the conspiratorial group dynamics within American politics. More recently, Volkan (2020) has contended that psychoanalytic training should include courses in large group dynamics in order for analysts to "have a serious voice in national and international affairs" (p. 115).

Since it is frustratingly apparent when dealing with true believers of what are verifiable lies and disinformation as well as outrageous conspiratorial theories, and because factual information fails to put the paranoid-minded individual into effective two-way communication (as in most intellectual exchange), the timeless and more autistic realm of fantasy needs to be appreciated in terms of fundamental, underlying fears and accompanying hatreds—namely, the archaic, primordial fears of annihilation and extinction. These must be understood, albeit oftentimes rather abstractly, and addressed as compassionately as possible. In order to focus on the social conditions mobilizing such paranoid thinking, it is important to identify with the *other*—and in particular, to be aware of one's own paranoid proclivities when one feels unseen, powerless, or oppressed.

Still, it is not so easy to identify with an individual or group *other*, one that—mainly through projective processes—experiences you or your group as demonically bad or evil. As analytic clinicians know from working with a psychotic transference in which the analyst fully inhabits being *the* "bad" object, it is enormously challenging to "*un-other* the Other" (Hoffman, 2021, p. 403, italics added). Yet, this is what is called for in order to contain the malignant forces in the polity. Because compassion in such circumstances is powerfully opposed by terrifying anxieties pertaining to the *other*, it is especially important to disentangle *normative, benign forms of othering* that begin with "stranger anxiety" in infancy, from *malignant, hateful othering* (cf. ibid.; Moss, 2021). It is the latter that is prominent through more destructively regressive large-group processes, as evident among many Trump followers (and somewhat less so among some anti-Trumpians).

From a Bionian group theory perspective, as discussed in Chapter 3, Chrzanowski (2019), in stressing tendencies to deny the role played by massive *regression* and *dissociation* in the total group situation (i.e., among both Trump supporters and his detractors), suggests that account must be taken of the *basic assumption phenomena* leading to regressive fantasies that a leader like Trump skillfully manipulates and reinforces through his oscillation between soothing, reassuring, and hopeful tactics, on the one hand, and provocative, divisive, paranoid, chaotic, and destructive actions, on the other. In essence, then, psychotic instabilities within group experience must no longer be denied, and instead, difficult work must be undertaken along the path from regression and dissociation to a "dominant work group mentality" (ibid., p. 728), one that is no longer so beset with illusions and delusional vulnerabilities. This requires that all of us live within the total group situation, ultimately, to "struggle to accommodate or reconcile the turbulence of its emotional life" (p. 728).

As I hope to have detailed, the possibility of impacting psychotic group functioning requires a sophisticated psychoanalytic understanding of the ways in which the group's defenses—including perverse disavowal or dissociation of reality, negative hallucination, splitting, projection, and delusional (conspiratorial) thought—serve to protect the group's members against more primitive, psychotic anxieties of a depressive and paranoid quality. In short, there is nothing "deplorable," "ignorant," or necessarily "power seeking" or "malevolent" in the identification with and attachment to Trumpism; instead, as with our patients who function from the paranoid/schizoid mode, the group's leader offers its members a *second skin* serving as a form of containment—albeit in a rotten, more perverted fashion—that is unconsciously motivated to defend "against anxieties whose sources could not be consciously controlled" (Jaques, 1955, p. 479).

Many of Trump's detractors have discovered, in line with Hannah Arendt's (1951) observations, that the conviction of ardently faithful adherents of totalitarian leaders cannot be altered by contrary evidence; in this context, the leader's "rotten" or "perverse" second skin serves as an impassable screen that protects against terrifying emotional experiences. Consequently, the intractability to change (seen, for instance, in continual refusal to accept verifiable truths that refute delusional conspiratorial beliefs), like the proverbial *negative therapeutic reaction*, can become both more understandable and potentially transformable once a healthier form of containment becomes possible. Such an outcome is most likely achieved—though far from easily realized—primarily through forging an alliance with healthy, sane elements (which must first be located) that open the possibility for change to occur.

Overall, successful interventions addressing conspiratorial thinking, often through the presentation of counter-conspiratorial information (utilized as inoculation prior to conspiratorial communications), while sometimes effective, may also backfire. Particularly among cultist, totalitarian groups, *faith* is rarely amenable to contrary information (Arendt, 1951; Loewenstein, 2018). Similarly, encouraging analytical rather than intuitive thinking may also be useful, but more research is necessary (Douglas et al., 2019). Besides psychoanalytically oriented insights that help in understanding and making contact with the "true believer," it may also be useful to employ psychologically based deprogramming methodologies.

Truth telling in the realm of delusional, conspiratorial thinking and cultist attachments

Lifton (2020) argues for hope that those whom he terms "witnessing professionals (and citizens)" will step forward in an effort to expose malignant normality and take a stand against it. In a related vein, Bollas (2020) recommends calling out the negative hallucinations that run rampant in psychotic group processes. More hopefully, much like the critical analytic thinkers of the Frankfurt School, Bollas believes that doing this can help "immunize" the public against destructive attacks on reality.

However, successful corrective actions against conspiratorial thinking are extremely difficult to accomplish, just as therapeutic work with delusional structures tends to be met with massive and often violent resistance. Especially when there is group support for such thinking, as apparent among conspiracy theorist members of QAnon, a group's true believer "is a hard man to change" (Festinger et al., 1956, p. 3). Because these beliefs tend to be largely rooted in unconscious emotional attachments rather than rational, intellectually based appraisal of evidence, the cooler hubris of analytic thinking must be held more lightly by those outside the conspiratorial bubble in order to find ways to connect to and possibly impact those within the bubble. In this respect, it can be useful to keep in mind that we ourselves may often hold beliefs for which, at least on the basis of logical argument, there is little or no compelling evidence.

Certainly, however, the function of the *third* in the body politic is crucial in order to reveal and expose conspiracies by identifying both delusional falsehoods and the individuals or groups who are enabling conspiratorial notions to take hold. While true believers may remain entrenched and virulently opposed to contradictory, verifiable information, their potency is more likely to be contained in an atmosphere in which attacks on truth are called out by a *relatively impartial third*. In the context of Trumpism, we see this happening when a moderate, centrist member of the Republican electorate, such as Mitt Romney, Ben Sasse, Adam Kinzinger, or Liz Cheney, speaks out against the leader's perverted rhetoric. In playing the role of the impartial third and inhabiting the symbolic function, such persons are better positioned to enable tensions between conspiracy and fact, madness and sanity, to be tolerated within the larger unit.

Esteemed political scientist Daniel Ziblatt (2017) observed that in twentieth-century Western societies such as Germany and Great Britain, and very much in accord with Hofstadter's (1965) studies, democracy's stability rests on a healthy conservative party's ability to regulate its extremist, reactionary factions most prone to conspiratorial beliefs and more violent intentions. As Jan-Werner Müller (2021) contends, "[W]hile everyone is entitled to their *opinions*, everyone cannot have their own *facts*" (p. 184, italics added). In short, the healthy sociopolitical contribution of conservative elites is crucial to preserving liberal democracy.

Keeping this in mind, truth telling by those outside the conspiratorial bubble or cult must be utilized as a tool or weapon of resistance to the blatant mendacity of Trumpist attacks on verifiable truth, as well as its persistent use of conspiratorial thinking. Due in part to our dependence on the internet and our avid, uncritical embrace of social media, we are living in what is rightfully considered a *post-truth era* in which the limits of the First Amendment are strikingly evident. Consequently, given today's slippery status of truth, it has become crucial to *speak truth to power*, while independent observers or witnessing professionals courageously seek and proclaim verifiable truth. Because social media and internet communication have become so prevalent in the distortion of truth, different approaches are being explored to deal with the agitating, emotionalizing propaganda and mendacity; for instance, a Norwegian website requires fact-based verification through responses to questioning before an article can be shared or commented upon (Skale, 2021). Increasing oversight pertaining to verifiable truth telling (and at least noting the lack thereof) by major websites such as Facebook, Twitter, YouTube, Instagram, and the like seems necessary in order to reestablish "rational thinking and interrupt emotional automatism" that is so prevalent among those individuals isolated in front of a screen (ibid., p. 243).

The effectiveness of truth telling often rests on what psychoanalysis reminds us to bear in mind and respect—namely, that truth is a tricky business that must often be approached ironically inasmuch as the need for illusion is ever-present (Steiner, 2020). Given unconscious resistances to change, deep-seated emotionally based group attachments, and multiple layers of reality, zealous truth telling can be too cruel to digest, so that "truth without kindness is not fully true" (p. 57). Arguably, then, when more psychoanalytically informed understanding, tact, and caution are brought to bear, such *truth telling and lie detection* becomes what Hannah Arendt (1951) described as the most effective weapon against totalitarianism, and what contemporary historian Sophia Rosenfeld (2019) regards as an essential "ethical and epistemological commitment" for those in public life (p. 160).

Although psychoanalytic expertise may be limited as a tool with which to impact the selection of effective political leaders, and despite the complexity of our selection processes, several analysts suggest that it may be feasible to bring psychoanalytic knowledge to bear in such selection. For instance, Kernberg (2020) speculates that analysts might critically evaluate the potential presence of necessary and optimal moderate levels of narcissistic and paranoid features (see also Volkan, 2020). Likewise, Bollas (2020) conjectures about the potential usefulness of drawing on mental health criteria to vet potential leadership.

Building bridges through meaningful intergroup contact

To restate some of these points in another way, we should keep in mind that interventions are necessary to enable a healthier, saner political frame that can retain the total group's sane elements (which exist in both populist sectors and more traditional democratic ones), while also managing its psychotic elements through facilitating intergroup contact. Spanning otherwise unbridgeable gaps between two or more individuals or groups frequently entails finding *commonalities*, which can often serve as the chief method by which empathy is aroused. The latter is accomplished largely by increasing understanding and compassion. Similarities and areas of overlap must be identified and brought forward, rather than maintaining a focus on differences and rigid borders that foment divisiveness and impassable divisions.

Malignant, hateful othering typified by murderous, annihilating impulses becomes less likely when benign forms of othering that encompass differences and regulate competitiveness are operative. In this way, the reductionistic dehumanization of otherness can be diminished, and others are more likely seen for who and what they are, not for what they evoke (Hoffman, 2021; Volkan, 2020). This is especially pertinent given the trend toward populist groups, which are prone to becoming destructively solipsistic. Tolerance in liberal democracies is best served by finding and encouraging shared common ground, and by supporting cultural and communal identities through rituals and other socially interactive processes—as are often found in the world of music and other performing and visual arts, in sports, entertainment, celebratory rites, and occasionally even in religion and war. Moreover, diverse factions can be brought together over time through both educational and civic approaches, as I will elaborate toward the end of this chapter.

In the markedly polarizing atmosphere in the US today, finding commonality also entails countering the dehumanization of members of the alt-right, believers of conspiracies, and ardent Trump supporters. It is especially important for psychoanalysts and other mental health professionals, along with social scientists, to tread lightly in utilizing data about descriptive personality trends among Trump supporters and those susceptible to conspiracy thinking. As clinicians well know, an overemphasis on personality traits, descriptive labels, and diagnostic categories is often counterproductive in furthering a dialogue between opposing factions. Moreover, the sense of having been wronged, of suffering from heightened levels of depressive and anxious mood, can be misused to distance oneself from, and even to dehumanize an individual, rather than leading toward connection with a human being who is suffering pain and is defending him- or herself in a particular way.

Rather than pejoratively *othering* by perniciously devaluing or maligning a specific group and its members, we must guard against any such tendency and instead make efforts to humanize. In this respect, the exercise of freedom in a democracy *cannot* be absolute given liberty's ongoing dialectic with equality and uncertainty. This is particularly so vis-à-vis the freedom to enact hatred through provocative—and at times even violence-inducing—demonization of others. Consequently, such freedoms require regulation in the sense that "people cannot have license to undermine … their fellow citizens as free and equal members of the polity" (Müller, 2021, p. 184).

We must keep in the forefront of our thinking that there are many ways to be human; a first step, as noted earlier in this chapter, is to recognize that there is nothing inherently "deplorable," "ignorant," "power-seeking," or "malevolent" in an identification with and attachment to Trump and his policies. Intrapsychic ambivalence concerning authoritarianism is ubiquitous as the human psyche unconsciously wrestles with conflicting impulses to seek refuge by embracing and caving in to authority, in opposition to aggressive, resisting forces toward individuation. For some, surrendering to a cult professing individual freedom that favors action instigated by *Newspeak* represents a *compromise formation*. Furthermore, there are many variations in ways of being political; for instance, it is important to appreciate that there is nothing intrinsically repugnant or evil in a predisposition to authoritarianism, nor intrinsically agreeable or good in its antithesis. As Wilkerson (2020), points out, there is a "greater sense of joint responsibility to one another when ... [individuals] see their fellow citizens *as like themselves*" (p. 353, italics added).

Nonetheless, the destructive populist dynamic is difficult to dissolve or loosen because paranoid projections and distorted perception, along with the seductive pull of perverted promises, must be disenchanted; this can be accomplished through constructive dialogue with individuals or groups trapped in destructive narcissism (Zienert-Eilts, 2020) and the alluring pull of eternal fascism (Eco, 1995). To restate some of these ideas in different terms, because utopian fantasies and illusions of unity and sameness, as well as the need for cohesion and belonging, are pervasive at both the right and left ends of the political spectrum, an especially useful and important pathway toward constructive change is to find ways to *identify with* the disappointed, albeit less fanatical members of the populist cult.

In order to move in this direction as an antidote to a *reverse psychoanalysis* (Adorno, 1951), psychoanalytic ethics requires that we become acquainted with the more pathological and at times conspiratorial, cultist, and fascist states of mind within ourselves (Loewenstein, 2020). This requires the protracted challenge of one's own psychic work to transform destructive anger and existential fears that increase susceptibility to authoritarian and fascist states of mind in a way that allows us to better understand these hard-to-digest processes (i.e., the longing for a container in its original, non-perverted form). For example, this might entail the common, universally empathized-with hope for a better future, particularly for one's children and grandchildren.

Oftentimes, a more radical form of empathy is vital in order to connect with the humanity of the other, much as has been suggested by a range of activist writers, including Fromm (1964), Hofstadter (1965), Volkan (2020), and Wilkerson (2020). In this type of empathy, courage and an awareness of the responsibility to undertake difficult psychic work are mobilized in order to understand someone else who may be vastly different from oneself in culture, caste, and experience, as well as in values, morals, and belief systems. Approaching this from a psychoanalytic perspective entails a radical and much more *receptive* form of listening—namely, *listening to* rather than *listening for*, or what Senator Angus King calls *eloquent listening.* Such listening incorporates a sense of reciprocity in which the thinking, feelings, and values of the other are paid attention to closely and receptively, entailing a radical openness. Despite manifest discord, prospects for change become more encouraging when there is a "personal stirring of empathy" (Rao, 2021, p. 418). In contrast to hope that is less realistically based (what might be termed "idle"), such personal empathy can access what has been called *practical hope*, which tends to promote positive action (Nussbaum, 2019, p. 206).

In examining seemingly unassailable divides and exploring possibilities for their eventual reconciliation, a noteworthy and very promising project termed "America in One Room" was carried out by Stanford scholars led by James Fishkin and colleagues (Fishkin et al., 2020), utilizing a method called *deliberative democracy* (Fishkin, 2018). This methodology entails holding informed and moderated discussions among polarized, representative groups of the American electorate in which the salient issues are the central focus, while potentially loaded words such as *Democrat*, *Republican*, *Trump*, and *Obama* are consciously avoided. Highly encouraging findings have been reported in that both Republicans and Democrats evidence significantly decreased polarization not only in policy attitudes, but also in affective divisiveness—undoubtedly by means of listening to one another as a means toward *benign othering* in a safely contained atmosphere, while remaining focused on finding common ground.

The leadership of the body politic can be a crucial factor by serving as a unifying example representing sanity in the form of liberal democratic values and truth telling, while eschewing divisive paranoid/schizoid mechanisms and more impulsive or psychotic behavior. If leaders function similarly to skillful psychoanalysts in the midst of a tempestuous, more psychotic transference (and countertransference), the temperature can be appropriately lowered, and fires fueled by the agitation of chaos, promoting conquest rather than coexistence, can be damped down. Fortunately for the US, it seems that Joe Biden and Kamala Harris represent such leaders, and each offers considerable promise in this respect.

Modifying sociocultural and economic conditions that increase susceptibility to large-group regressions

As indicated in Chapter 2, the conditions that render individual Americans particularly susceptible to becoming part of large-group regressions include issues of caste, economic inequalities, social injustices, and threats to status. Consequently, it is necessary to address and *unmask* these conditions and the individuals, groups, and systems that perpetuate them, utilizing some sort of public accounting of the injustices.

In brief, it is important to expose those elements that render pernicious effects both in the subordinate and dominant castes and in the socioeconomic classes that make up the in- and out-groupings (Wilkerson, 2020). To make changes in this realm necessitates actively dealing with the conditions that foment terrifying existential anxieties, rage, and despair on both the left and right sides of the political spectrum—in particular, the injustices and inequities that have deepened the divide over the last forty to fifty years. As a familiar slogan states, "no justice, no peace"—or, in Martin Luther King, Jr.'s words (uttered in 1967 outside a California prison where Vietnam War protesters were being held): "There can be no justice without peace, and there can be no peace without justice."

Civil or "democratic" disobedience is essential in the face of rising authoritarianism, both in the US and worldwide (Müller, 2021). Such controlled law-breaking is much like what Martin Luther King, Jr., encouraged in the form of *loving* disobedience of unjust laws, and what Congressman and activist John Lewis endorsed in suggesting that *good trouble* is necessary. Such civilized resistance and activism are characterized by non-violence, conscientiousness, and the effort to convincingly persuade fellow citizens that unjust, unequal laws and practices must be changed (ibid.). Social science findings have shown that such non-violent disobedience is twice as likely as more violent approaches to meet the goal of producing fundamental political change (Chenoweth & Stephan, 2013).[1]

---

[1] In studying the impact of both non-violent and violent forms of resistance in different historical periods and geographical contexts over more than 100 years (from 1900 to 2006), Chenoweth and Stephan (2013) found that *non-violent resistance* presents fewer obstacles to moral and physical involvement and commitment. Moreover, higher levels of participation with the former contributed to enhanced resilience, greater opportunities for tactical innovation and peaceful civic disruption (and therefore less incentive for a regime to maintain its status quo), and an increased chance of shifts in loyalty among opponents' erstwhile supporters, including members of the military establishment. In short, these authors concluded that successful non-violent resistance leads to more durable and internally peaceful democracies, which are less likely to regress into civil war; consequently, violent insurgency is not justifiable on strategic grounds.

In recognizing the challenges that must be faced in order to address and hopefully alter malignant dynamics, Isabel Wilkerson (2020) suggests that the destructiveness of a "charismatic demigod" (such as Hitler and, by implication, Trump and his more militant followers) requires considerable courage to see the evil—or more aptly, the *banality of evil* (Arendt, 1963)—for what it is. Nonetheless, particularly for those outside the bubble of Trumpism, it remains important (albeit difficult) that such outsiders are able to identify with and carry compassion for the followers and enablers of such cult leaders *without absolving* inexcusable behavior. This can require "the courage to *stand up to the multitudes* in the face of a charismatic demigod who makes you feel better about yourself, part of something bigger than yourself, that you have been primed to believe" (Wilkerson, 2020, p. 266, italics added).

The rage experienced in those outside the Trump bubble, the anti-Trumpists and never-Trumpists, is more likely to attenuate when justice is served—in short, when there are serious consequences for the anti-democratic and criminal actions perpetrated by Trump and many of his enablers. Unfortunately, there is often considerable resistance to such accountability; we saw this, for instance, in the failure to secure a conviction for Trump's second impeachment, senatorial censure, conviction for criminal activities, and censure or banishment of Congress members who participated in insurgencies and other anti-constitutional activities, as well as those blatantly advocating voter suppression or engaging in QAnon-type conspiratorial thinking. We might take more hope, however, from recognizing that the seductive power of the destructive populist leader tends to actually decrease during *real* threats, such as the persisting COVID-19 crisis, as well as climate change and economic challenges—so that the reality principle inspired by increasing opposition and demographic patterns can gain ground.

In sum, to effectively deal with the conditions that have led to destructive forms of Trumpist populism, we do not need to focus on returning to our imaginary, fantasized past—a more or less pre-Trump "normal." Rather, we need to take a more realistic accounting of what is happening today in the context of a future-oriented reimagination, one that entails coming up with less nostalgic descriptions of aspirational ideals, morality, and work-oriented ingenuity. In Trump's America, this might entail something like a "Truth and Reconciliation Commission"

(Wilkerson, 2020) in the context of finding the shared ground that impacts all sides of the political spectrum—namely, a common ground in which to deal with agreed-upon societal ills, including immigration policy, infrastructure, economic inequities, and climate change.

Reestablishing and maintaining democracy's necessary social/institutional frame, second skin, or container

To reestablish and maintain a healthier institutional frame requires that political and social methods be employed to strengthen the role of the overseeing third in the form of important checks and balances, primarily within Congress and the judiciary—those that reinforce truth seeking, as well as adherence to standards, law, and norms in the political arena, while attenuating the role of power-seeking, anti-democratic individuals and movements that inhabit and fuel the psychotic element within the group. A healthy democracy requires that its intermediary institutions stand up to the polity's anti-democratic actors who fail to fully subscribe to the collective democratic project, especially those who seek to disenfranchise citizens or even to oppose the constitution itself (Müller, 2021). Political parties and the professional media require regulation in order to fulfill the crucial infrastructural functions that are necessary within a representative democracy. In short, America's *intermediaries* must remain accountable, as well as accurate, accessible, and autonomous; consequently, for many politicians and others serving this function, it is necessary to have the courage to be confrontational "without violating democratic standards" (ibid., p. 45).

The turbulence accompanying Trump's and his followers' attacks on liberal democracy, as well as the actions occurring among Trumpism's more radical factions, indicates the importance of recognizing the extreme precariousness of democracy and how easily it can break down when it is taken wholly for granted, and when what is crucial to its preservation is overlooked. Consequently, there needs to be little or no tolerance from intermediaries, such as elected officials, the media, and the judiciary, for marginalizing some citizens as *other*—as somehow second class or as not belonging based on their exclusion from the dominant group.

A key psychoanalytic concept that addresses the opening up of a space for symbolic function—a thinking space necessary for healthy functioning—is the vital importance of the *third* (*triangulation*). This phenomenon and its actualization in the nation's functioning remains critical for maintaining the necessary institutional containment—despite Trump's and his acolytes' relentless attacks on those entities representing thirdness, such as a truth-seeking media and an impartial judiciary.

In general, this requires reinforcing the *third* in various ways, most significantly in affirming democratic institutions through engagement and action in order to eschew the destruction of democracy. More specifically, such activities involve unmasking and actively opposing such extreme right-wing "big lies" as the 2020 presidential election having been "stolen", or that the January 6 insurrection was a harmless, innocent protest by true patriots riled up by Nancy Pelosi or Antifa, and as such it does not merit an independent investigation. Overall, then, the critical infrastructure of democracy itself needs to be strengthened, while—much as in psychoanalysis itself—a credible commitment to objectivity (though not necessarily neutrality) must be maintained at the same time (Müller, 2021). Accordingly, the media that trades in hyperbole and conspiracy requires a thoughtful "repluralization" in which there is a greater commitment to facts for the public good (Snyder, 2021). Techniques and processes used within the Trumpism bubble to perpetuate misinformation and lies—such as "what aboutism" and the use of projective identification—need to be called out in straightforward language.

For those not already familiar with the term, incidentally, *what aboutism* refers to a rhetorical technique made famous by the Soviets in which challenges are responded to by accusing the questioner of hypocrisy (often using moral equivalence); in addition, *projective identification* in the political sphere becomes another similarly used rhetorical technique that relies on splitting off and expelling undesirable, "bad" parts of oneself or one's group and locating them into the denigrated and disempowered other.

Moreover, from a more objective standpoint, it is necessary to place checks and regulatory limitations on anti-democratic members of Congress, and to stop enabling corporate sponsorship where post-truths are used for power and capitalistic gains. Realistic standards and legal parameters are essential, particularly for big donors and for individuals with large platforms and media sites who authorize "big lies" and make it possible for them to take hold (and even to foment insurrection).

Once again, this requires activism characterized by a willingness to push back at those leaders, officials, enablers, and media personalities who aggressively seek to further divide and polarize as well as to create chaos that can enhance their own power, fame, and/or wealth.[2]

Opposition to the authoritarian appeal of populist leaders like Trump and the seductiveness of Trumpian cultism requires that other societal factions skillfully address members of the polity in ways that assert the importance and value of democratic pluralism. This longer-range approach might involve an increasing emphasis on both early and secondary education in civics, as well as courses on news literacy (contra misinformation and "fake" news) and in democracy itself (such as the understandings that immigrants must master in order to become US citizens). In all such areas, careful attention must be paid to empowering students with the skills necessary for critical thinking. Moreover, in the long term, it is necessary to bring together members of younger generations that represent diverse groupings—especially millennials and post-millennials of Generation Z and beyond.

One approach promoting commonality through shared effort might be to require some form of service for one to two years, such as a "mandatory program of youth national civil service" (Nussbaum, 2018, p. 242).[3] As an antidote to hateful forms of othering the *other* through

---

[2] Political observers such as historian Timothy Snyder (2021) are encouraged by the increasing divides in the Republican Party that may better preserve democracy. For instance, the Mitch McConnell faction that seeks to maintain power by taking advantage of loopholes within the democratic system—in contrast to those who seem more willing to seize power by actually destroying the system, such as Ted Cruz and Josh Hawley—might return to more actively utilizing *policy* rather than mendacity and conspiratorial propaganda in order to win elections.

[3] Many countries, including those as dissimilar as France, Nigeria, and the Philippines, employ some form of voluntary or mandatory national civic service that does not necessarily involve military service. For instance, in a democracy much like that of the US, France has utilized *Service Civique* (the French National Volunteer Service) since 1995, in which *voluntary* commitment is open to those between the ages of sixteen and twenty-five, the duration of which can be six to twelve months. This program offers a state-provided allowance for community work assignments that are recognized as a national priority; areas of assignment include health and environmental education, dissemination of sciences and culture, civil defense and security, and promotion of Francophone and European citizenship. In 2019, French President Emmanuel Macron

close contact across race, gender, ethnicity, religion, socioeconomic status, and even age lines, such group service could bring together diverse individuals through work that encompasses younger citizens representing urban and rural settings, politically liberal and conservative persons, those of varied economic means, and educated "elites" and "real" people.

For instance, such service might involve working in healthcare, disability and eldercare facilities, providing teaching, mentoring, and educational aid, becoming directly involved in supporting the homeless and aiding in the mental health crises, assisting in the construction of low-income housing, and actively informing and helping citizens to utilize their civic rights and responsibilities (including voting). The overall goal, of course, is to address both the domestic and international challenges that the US faces today (Packer, 2021a).

Lifton (2020) is fairly optimistic in proposing an antidote to the current destructive cultism in the US. In thinking more along psychoanalytic lines, his hopefulness is based on the basic structure of the human mind in the form of a *protean, resilient, and multi-sided self* that resists a monolithic and unbending, cultist self—and a *symbolizing self* that seeks signification beyond simple signs that fail to capture the basic need for living in truth. Though the ubiquitous cultist, mad aspects of American culture won't ever be eradicated, containment seems more likely with the knowledge of how these processes operate.

---

implemented the *Service National Universel* (General National Service) as a civil conscription that has become mandatory for all male and female citizens aged sixteen to twenty-five (starting in 2021, with full implementation in 2026). This compulsory service lasts for only a month and can be performed in both civil and military facilities; moreover, its completion will be necessary in order for young persons to receive the *Baccalauréat* (the university-entrance diploma) and to undertake a driving license examination.

CHAPTER 7

Concluding thoughts: a plea for hope in these uncertain times

> *However uncertain I may ... remain as to whether we can hope for anything better for mankind, this uncertainty cannot detract ... from the necessity of assuming for practical purposes that human progress is possible. This hope for better times to come, without which an earnest desire to do something useful for the common good would never have inspired the human heart, has always influenced the activities of right-thinking men.*
>
> —Immanuel Kant (1793)

Steadying the bough during stormy seas that might cause the cradle to fall and the baby to tumble down, as in the dark nursery rhyme, is an apt metaphor for what our nation is facing today. As I've detailed in the foregoing chapters, this steadying requires reestablishment of the required container that can capably hold both the nation's mad parts and its sane ones. This enormous challenge entails calling out both the psychological dimensions and the pathogenic states of mind of the political and large-group process, while nonetheless embodying a humane, compassionate attitude toward those unconsciously entangled in malignant group processes.

Conflict, activism, and realistic hope

As addressed throughout this book, conflict and uncertainty are inevitable in a pluralistic society such as we enjoy in the US today. Moreover, because our democratic political process is in danger of breaking apart during these turbulent times, a central aim of this book is to provide psychoanalytically sound and interdisciplinary based understandings that can help us chart a realistically hopeful path forward. There is little reason to be optimistic if we merely stick to imagining favorable outcomes or subscribing to utopian fantasies—which, as psychoanalysis reminds us, easily leads to despair. As suggested in Chapter 6, I agree with the viewpoint expressed by distinguished philosopher Martha Nussbaum (2018) that hopefulness on the political front cannot remain inert or idle; instead, it requires action and commitment. In brief, hope must be grounded in practical reality, and it must be firmly held if we are to energize a commitment to action (ibid.). As the flip side of fear (as conveyed in Kant's sage epigraph to this chapter), hope is *a choice* that one can make—and indeed, a choice that one *must* make for the public good.

To restate an essential point, it is necessary that we actively work to establish and maintain *standards of accountability* for political figures. Just as when working with a mad, "psychotic," malignantly paranoid state of mind in a patient characterized by a violent, insurgent element, it is necessary in large-group settings to establish contact with the "sane" part of the group's mind. This is often accomplished by utilizing the equivalent of a metaphorical bridge (i.e., an alliance) that enables the psychotic element to be contained and managed by this healthier element, which can recognize and listen to the "mad" element. In particular, as I've stated, we require a healthier, more "sane" *third* to serve as a "good enough" container, second skin, or frame that subsumes various contrasting political values and yet remains attuned to the humanity of all the group's members.

It is important to note, however, that an Enlightenment perspective favoring reasoning as the primary source of authority and legitimacy, aspiring to intellectual progress, is largely characteristic of the academic thinking that has so profoundly influenced the many interdisciplinary contributors to this volume. Nonetheless, as I've argued throughout the book, because of the dialectical nature of America's liberal democracy, and despite the considerable scholarship and insight that most interdisciplinary scholars have offered—as did, for example, Immanuel Kant in this chapter's epigraph on "right thinking"—such Enlightenment reasoning remains necessary yet insufficient to address and contain the fundamental tensions of democracy's conflicts and uncertainty. Instead, it is necessary to supplement its intellectual ideals with psychoanalytic thinking that arguably can enable greater access to and success in dealing with the primitive, non-rational, and unconscious forces that operate within the polity.

Within our democratic, pluralistic culture, perhaps the most sizeable—and crucial—societal challenge is to recognize and "address the emotional needs of vulnerable communities who have differing values and … needs and who may view themselves in competition with one another" (Hoffman, 2018, p. 284). Perhaps only in this context, in which the basic social-emotional needs of so many are attended to, can the malignant members' psychotic element be managed, promoting the group's enduring survival through the successful titration of overpowering forms of conflict and division.

As I've argued, however, the more extreme forms of populism evident in Trumpist America are not surprising when a large segment of the public lacks trust in the fundamental impartiality, commitment to truth, and fairness of the institutions that have the potential to contain democracy's inherent tensions. This is especially so when a significant segment of the population fails to benefit from the prevailing economic conditions and feels that the elites are excessively profiting from having the upper hand. Such socioeconomic conditions also contribute to festering resentments against the "other"—those viewed as "less than" the established mainstream population (e.g., people of color, persons who are physically or mentally handicapped, LGBTQ-identified, etc.)—leading to a rise in hate crimes and other violence against targeted groups, who are seen as stealing resources (jobs, social benefits, medical care, etc.) from the middle group.

Under these circumstances, democracy's institutions and intermediaries *must* mediate and resolve conflicts between the people and the state and between various factions of the population. However, the democratic process itself is placed in great danger when a strongman such as Trump—much like Erdoğan in Turkey, Orbán in Hungary, or Duterte in the Philippines—claims to support the people in standing up to the elites, and then asks to relax the established, necessary institutional checks and balances so that, ostensibly, he can better serve the people (Acemoglu & Robinson, 2020).

The illusion of unity amid turbulence

Whereas psychoanalytic thought cannot be turned into an explanation for everything, a sort of all-encompassing psychology, psychoanalytic understanding—as I have elaborated in this book—is nonetheless uniquely situated both to appreciate and to counter wishful, utopian, and omnipotent fantasies and illusions of unity that reside in the nation's psyche. As psychoanalysts know very well, however, the need for illusion is ubiquitous, and to some extent an appeal to the illusion of unity may have helped Joe Biden win the 2020 presidential election, especially through pleas to recover "the soul of America." This tactic brings to mind Abraham Lincoln's remarks in his first inaugural address of 1861, when, in facing America's "exceptionalism" and "sinfulness," he called upon "the better angels of our nature."

While of course there are "better angels" in the US, it is essential to appreciate that the nation's psyche, or soul, is riddled with fissures and splits whose containment is inherently perilous. We are a country of a great many divisions, a country that is "neither a land of the free and home of the brave nor a bastion of white supremacy … Rather, it is both, and other things as well" (Packer, 2021b, p. 190). Consequently, unity is not necessarily a strength as an operative feature in America's liberal democracy, whose very existence depends on diversity and multiculturalism within the masses, in which differences are held in tension. Moreover, as I've discussed in relation to individuals and groups with a more authoritarian predisposition, the movement toward unity in the face of multiculturalism and diversity is anathema (Applebaum, 2020; Stenner, 2005; Stenner & Haidt, 2018).

Democracy requires participation and effort from its citizens, as well as a certain level of "tolerance for cacophony and chaos" (Applebaum, 2020, p. 189; see also S. Rosenfeld, 2019). As politically oriented economists Daron Acemoglu and James Robinson (2020) suggest, there is a "narrow corridor to liberty" (p. xvii) in which we aim for sufficient balancing of conflicts and cooperation between the public (i.e., *society*) and the government (i.e., the *state*) to permit us to tolerate the discordance of liberal democracy. It is this "corridor" that stands between the fears and repression of despotic states and the lawlessness and violence that emerge among the people when the state is entirely absent. Many observers maintain that because so many individuals—by some accounts, roughly a third of the American people—are greatly challenged by diversity and dissimilarities that seem threatening, changes that throw these elements into high relief become increasingly difficult to stomach (Stenner, 2005; Stenner & Haidt, 2018). Moreover, as divisiveness, differences, and chaos have continued to mount in what seems an ever-narrowing corridor, Stenner and Haidt (2018) contend that "Western liberal democracies have now exceeded many people's capacity to tolerate them" (p. 209). While this is undoubtedly partially true, I suggest that the "people's" capacity for containment rests on widening the corridor and strengthening the container through a more nuanced understanding of unconscious group processes and the inevitability of malignant forms of regression.

America's ability to strengthen the container and widen the corridor when its democratic institutions have become gridlocked, when they may not be up to the task, is greatly hindered by faux notions of the country's unity among its diverse factions. In contrast, a more efficacious container needs to encompass competition and yet further encourage cooperation between the large group's populist factions and the governmental and societal elites. Interestingly and somewhat paradoxically, more malignant populist groupings, typified by Trumpism, are joining together in an illusion of unity in opposition to being forced to come together with, or integrated in unity with, diversified *others*. In a strange irony, although many feel a sense of commonality and belonging in considering Trump their leader, Trump is actually a great unifier of otherwise opposing factions; he has brought together many diverse groups who had been unaware of their "mutual affinity—bankers and neo-Nazi thugs, tech bros and peddlers of deranged conspiracy theories" (O'Toole, 2021, p. 9).[1]

More disturbingly in view of Trump's failed coup attempt of 2020–2021, and as noted in Chapter 6, today's Trump-supporting Republican Party has become a coalition of two very distinct segments: *gamers* such as Mitch McConnell, the "gamer in chief," who seeks to "game" the system to maintain power and take advantage of constitutional obscurities; and *breakers* like Ted Cruz and Josh Hawley, who appear willing to actually "break" or destroy the system in order to attain power *without democracy* (Snyder, 2021). Accordingly, and arguably in an even more derisive voice, political philosopher Jan-Werner Müller (2021) casts Republican voters as themselves more likely to fall into becoming either "suckers" or "scoundrels."

While arguing against such reductive descriptions of large swaths of humanity belonging to the Trumpian world, this book has also addressed the fact that any proposed changes in the malignant group's relationship to truth and a sane mode of processing can be expected to be met with impenetrable and possibly even violent resistances that serve to preserve defenses, such as splitting, projection, and delusional thinking. Here the emergence of psychotic anxieties and the group's madness is inevitable. Nonetheless, the key to restoring verifiable truth to its rightful status among members of the malignant group rests partly on courageous actions and words put forward by the democratic, supporting *third*—a feat not easily achieved in the current era. Indeed, as *The Washington Post*'s motto puts it, "Democracy dies in darkness."

However, rather than being blinded by the dark, as this book's epigraph implies, we have the opportunity to meet and get to know our shadows in the deepening shade. For psychoanalysts, the dark side is

---

[1] Despite the fact that Trump's ardent followers span a very wide gamut from far-right extremists and conspiracy theorists to "country club" Republicans and non-English-speaking immigrants, an assumption frequently shared by those on the political left and the right is that social factions or groups vote in particular, predictable ways. This problematic form of stereotyping, termed *democratic determinism* (Müller, 2021), does not allow for the unexpected or for changing needs, ideas, and voting choices; an unfortunate consequence is that useful activism can easily be considered essentially powerless to effect change.

often encountered in the shaded hues of one's dreams—both the dreams of patients and those of the analyst.

A second dream of mine: an appeal for curious inquiry and compassion?

Just prior to submitting this book's final manuscript for publication in the late summer of 2021, I had a second dream in which Trump appeared in my office. However, the underlying tone was quite distinct from that of my 2017 nightmarish dream described in my Author's Preface, in which I felt helplessly bullied by Trump's ruthless and brazen belligerence. As noted in the Preface, only recently have I come to understand the first dream as an unconscious portent to my developing a book that reflects my own "psychoanalysis" of America's relationship to Trump and Trumpism.

In contrast, however, the more recent dream had a far more benign quality. In this dream, Trump was again my patient, but rather than feeling useless and angry—and while fully recognizing his pugnacious, disturbing way of being—I nonetheless awoke feeling surprised by my very curious attitude throughout the dream. Rather than demonizing this well-known figure who had unexpectedly turned up on my couch, I found myself seeking to understand what might lie beneath his disruptive and dangerous bravado. Moreover, I was astounded to realize that I felt compassion and an unbidden empathy for this man who was clearly so fragile and broken.

In reflecting further, I found myself wondering if the process of writing this book had actually changed something deep within me—much as a successful psychoanalytic process can effect profound change for patient and analyst alike—though hopefully *not* to the extent of absolving Trump's inexcusable behavior (nor that of his followers). I believe my unconscious was reminding me that, as an outside observer tackling the putatively evil elements emanating from a regressed, cultist group (one too easily rendered as *other*), I am required to do a great deal more than simply examine how such malevolent processes can take hold. In short, in order to contain a group's malignancies, it is essential—just as it is for a skilled psychoanalyst treating a patient's primitive psychopathology—that an attitude of *curious exploration* of unconscious dynamics be accompanied by a significant measure of *compassion* for individuals who function within the regressed group mentality.

Some reflections in closing

When we meet our shadows in the deepening shade, realistic, practical hope ascends if we are able to remain vigilant, organized, and politically active in widening the container to encompass discordance, including malignancies in the large-group psyche. Liberal democracy, founded on the principles of liberty and equality, can be maintained and flourish only when both the state and its citizens can remain strong enough to promote "a mobilized society that participates in politics, protests when it is necessary, and votes the government out of power when it can" (Acemoglu & Robinson, 2020, p. xvii).

Yet perhaps more so at the present time than has ever been the case in American history, it is crucial to realize that utopian fantasies are counterproductive, that reliance on reason alone is insufficient, and that *apathy kills. Activism* leavened by curiosity and nuanced understanding of what is being dealt with, combined with a measure of compassion for the terrified "other" caught up in the large group's malignant web, is crucial. Thus, for psychoanalysts and others interested in recognizing, coming to understand, and working with the unconscious "mad" aspects of the nation's social and political factions, this is a time when it is vital to mobilize such inquisitiveness and concern in order to make what the late Georgia congressman and civil rights leader John Lewis called *good trouble, necessary trouble.*

Glossary

Terms and concepts that refer to political and psychoanalytic ideas are used in various contexts in a multitude of ways, and confusion inevitably arises from the lack of agreed-upon meanings and the concepts to which they refer, particularly when words are used idiosyncratically or imprecisely. Consequently, as an aid to the reader, in this section I state specifically what I mean when I use these terms in this book. I ask the reader to keep in mind, however, that other writers may use the same terms and ideas with different nuances, and sometimes even with different meanings.

Alpha function is psychoanalyst Wilfred Bion's designation for the mental activity operating on sense impressions and felt affect that is essential for the reception, elaboration, and communication of our experiences, which in turn create the basis for feeling, thinking, and dreaming. It is the cornerstone of the acceptance and knowledge of reality, and when it fails to operate in what we might consider a "normal" way, sense impressions and subjective feelings remain in their pre-cognate, unrepresentable state.

Authoritarianism is a form of government characterized by the rejection of political plurality. Authoritarianism favors the use of a strong central power to preserve the political status quo, as well as reductions in the rule of law, separation of powers, and democratic voting.

Autocracy is an illiberal, one-party system of government in which supreme power over a state is concentrated in the hands of one person, whose decisions are subject neither to external legal restraints nor to regularized mechanisms of popular control. It serves as a mechanism for holding power and functions alongside leftist or rightist ideologies, often permitting limited or token opposition.

Basic assumption group refers to Bionian-studied group phenomena in which members of the group share basic assumptions that arise out of intense and primitive emotions. These assumptions impact the group's culture and functioning in establishing beliefs about three basic factors: *dependence*, implying a collective belief in a protective deity (leader or institution) that provides security; *fight/flight*, implying the existence of an external enemy that must be avoided or vanquished; and *pairing*, in which there is an implicit, hopeful belief for a future messiah who will solve all the group's problems.

Compromise formation is an attempt to resolve an internal conflict that provides an acceptable degree of partial expression for each of the psyche's competing forces or parties to the conflict. These intrapsychic compromises allow competing forces, such as frequently occur among wishes, impulses, and defenses, to reconcile by meeting again in something of a middle ground, as expressed in actions, symptoms, dreams, slips of the tongue, or other modes of expression.

Conservatism is a political and social philosophy opposing rapid change and promoting traditional social institutions. In Western culture, conservatives typically seek to preserve a range of democratic institutions such as organized religion, parliamentary government, and property rights.

Conspiracy, also known as a plot, is a secret plan or agreement between persons (called conspirers or conspirators) for an unlawful or harmful purpose, such as murder or treason, especially with political motivation, while keeping their agreement secret from the public and/or from those affected by it. In its political sense, it suggests a group of conspirators united in the aim of altering, usurping, or overthrowing an established political power, typically through wrongdoing or illegal means.

Conspiracy theory is an assumption or set of beliefs that rejects the standard or unexplained account for an event, and instead credits a covert group or organization for carrying out a secret, deceptive, and nefarious plot.

Container/contained, a notion derived by Wilfred Bion from the Kleinian concept of *projective identification*, represents the apparatus of thinking that enables psychic growth. It serves as the basis of any relationship between two or more people, including an individual and a group or society. The *container* receives projections and employs alpha functioning to arrange and return them in a useful form that enables thinking and growth to occur.

Containment occurs when the container (i.e., the containing object) is able to titrate, translate, and metabolize the other's (or the group's) projected, weakly represented sensory and emotional material (beta products) through successful alpha functioning.

Delusion refers to an internal experience appearing in the perceptual field; in short, it arises from inside one's mental life but appears to the subject as external to the self, so that the whole of reality is affected. Freud believed that delusions reflect belief in an alternative "fantasy reality" when aspects of external, consensual reality are too psychically threatening; in such situations, there is an attempt to force perceptions to support such beliefs so that fantasy becomes reality. Consequently, a flexible, "normal" relationship between reality and truth is disrupted.

Democracy means rule by the people and is a system of government by the whole population or all the eligible members of a state, typically through elected representatives. The people take part in decisions that affect them, while the right and power to rule is granted by democratic forms of competition. Essentially, the people have the authority to choose their governing legislators, especially when rule is determined by a majority of the people. In a *representative democracy*, such as the United States, the people elect representatives to deliberate and decide on legislation, and its successful functioning requires a loyal opposition to the government in power without denying its legitimacy (in short, *not* an opposition to the democratic political system itself). This is also the case in *presidential* (or *parliamentary*) *democracy*. In contrast, in a *direct democracy*, the people directly deliberate and decide on legislation.

Demophobia refers to an abnormal fear of masses of people or crowds; it is used in the political sphere (across the political spectrum) to mean fear of ordinary people and of the freedom to vote. It may manifest in social or political groups when others who are perceived as a threat to one's own group's survival become demonized and are viewed as unworthy of participating in a democratic system.

Denial, which is often termed *disavowal*, refers to an unconscious defense mechanism by which psychic distress is reduced by repudiating awareness of a painful, external reality, and/or there is a frank refusal to accept painful or uncomfortable internal reality. It frequently takes the form of unconsciously rejecting the meaning of a reality-based event or its perception, especially in traumatic situations. While moderate levels of denial are normative and healthy, its persistence and intensity typically reflect something more problematic—particularly when a large group tenaciously holds to such disavowal and therefore functions through meta-denial to "deny the denial."

Depressive position (D) is psychoanalyst Melanie Klein's term for the developmental achievement and psychic stance or position that integrates love and hate for objects, their "good" and "bad" aspects and other partial representations, and external reality with intrapsychic reality and fantasy. In contrast to the *paranoid–schizoid position (P/S)*, the *depressive position (D)* arises when aggression is no longer wholly projected outward, and the capacity for concern for the object, reparative tendencies, and genuine love become attainable, and humility and gratitude are more likely. This position (D) oscillates with the P/S stance and remains a transient state of mind.

Ego ideal is a Freudian concept referring to the psychic structure that depicts the image of oneself as one wants to be. It tends to be formed through representations based on identifications (with idealized parents and other significant figures, as well as with early self-images). This notion enriches the understanding of group psychology in that a collective ideal supersedes the individual ego ideal that has been projected onto the group. The structure itself serves as a gauge with which to assess how well the individual or group has met their expectations.

Fascism is an extreme form of authoritarian ultra-nationalism characterized by dictatorial power, forcible suppression of opposition, and strong regimentation of society and of the economy. It came to prominence in parts of early twentieth-century Europe and, as a form of extreme nationalism, it ultimately takes on the contours of whatever national culture produces it, though it tends to involve mass mobilization and militarization of entire societies in modern authoritarian populist states. Fascist movements are characterized by the belief in a natural social hierarchy, extreme militaristic nationalism, and the subordination of individual interests to the good of the nation; consequently, it is marked by contempt for electoral democracy as well as for political and cultural liberalism.

Identification is a mature form of internalization that refers to the unconscious mental processes by which an individual becomes like another in one or more aspects. It refers to the process that brings into the psyche the less concrete (and often role-oriented) aspects of significant others in relation to oneself.

Identity politics refers to a political approach and form of activism wherein people of a particular gender, religion, race, social background, class, or other identification develop political agendas based on the group members having been impacted by systems of oppression. Though individuals may adopt the term to demonstrate that they belong to the *real people*, it actually refers to social differences that are used politically in order to gain empowerment as well as to address societal injustices; in the US, it is usually ascribed to oppressed groups who are fighting discrimination.

Liberal democracy is a political ideology and a form of government in which representative democracy operates under the principles of liberalism. It is generally understood to be a system of government in which people give consent to their rulers, and rulers are constitutionally constrained to respect and protect individual rights (though widely divergent views exist regarding the meaning of individual rights and constraints). It is characterized by elections of individuals representing multiple distinct political parties, a separation of powers into different branches of government, the rule of law in everyday life as part of an open society, a market economy with private property, and the equal protection of human rights, civil rights, civil liberties, and political freedoms for all people. In contrast, an *illiberal democracy* has weak or no limits on the power of the elected representatives to rule as they please.

Malignant narcissism is a severe form of pathological narcissism. It is a type of narcissistic personality disorder that combines narcissistic and paranoid traits in which unconscious conflicts around intense aggressive affect are dominant, in combination with and infiltrating the compensatory grandiose self. Aggression becomes ego-syntonic, and paranoid tendencies ensue from its projection. Deficits in moral functioning and in ethical superego structures commonly produce antisocial behaviors.

Manichean psychology denotes a dualistic view of human behavior that focuses on a life-and-death struggle between two opposing sides—namely, a good, spiritual world of light that contrasts with an evil, material world of darkness. The term *Manichean* is often used figuratively as a synonym for philosophical or a worldview's "dualism" in which everything is broken down into good or evil.

Meritocracy is a political system in which economic goods and/or political power are vested in individual people on the basis of talent, effort, and/or achievement, rather than according to wealth or social class. Advancement in such a system is based on performance, as measured through examination or demonstrated achievement. In the United States, meritocracy's anti-democratic character arises from unequal access to opportunity that creates increasing inequality, and arguably, a decline of the middle class.

Monarchy is a form of government in which an individual person—the monarch—is head of state for life or until abdication. The political legitimacy and authority of the monarch may vary from purely symbolic, to restricted, to fully autocratic, and can expand across executive, legislative, and judicial domains.

Negative capability refers to psychoanalyst Wilfred Bion's use of John Keats's (1817) notion that involves the ability to place oneself in the position of *not knowing* in order to receive what remains unknown. Keats described this as: "capable of being in uncertainty, mysteries, and doubts, without any irritable reaching after fact and reason … capable of remaining content with half knowledge" (pp. 477–478). Apropos of one of the demands of democracy, it is a form of thinking and being that supports permitting whatever is uncertain to remain so.

Neoliberalism connotes a conception of freedom as an overarching social value associated with reducing state functions and privatizing public economic sectors or services. As a laissez-faire or free-market ideology that forms the dominant political and sociocultural system in most of today's Western democracies, it is characterized by deregulation and marketization in which economic and social policies are especially congenial to corporations, with limited regard for personal consequences.

Normative threat is a term used by social scientists in studying large groups to refer to the perception of frightening societal conditions frequently activated by more profound social transformations, especially when there are significant perceived failures in societal consensus, leadership, and institutional trust. When such fears become particularly terrifying in existential ways (often exacerbated by demagoguery), authoritarian trends, conspiratorial thinking, and resistances to interpersonal differences tend to increase, creating further polarization within the larger polity.

Oligarchy is a form of power structure in which power rests with a small number of people. These designated rulers may be distinguished by, for example, nobility or wealth. In general, wealthy rulers attempt to ensure personal benefit from political decisions and to rule according to their own solipsistic agendas, to the point of avarice. In the United States, oligarchs tend to align with an increasingly radicalized right.

Paranoia is one of the oldest concepts in the history of describing mental states that derive from the mental activity known as *projection* of split-off aspects of the self. It is recognizable in group processes by the tendency to narcissistically invest in and idealize one's own group and to distrust, as well as to project hostility and evil into, those outside the group.

Paranoid–schizoid position (P/S) refers to the Kleinian psychoanalytic idea of the first and most primitive organization of the mental apparatus, which continues to exert influence throughout life in a dynamic relationship with the depressive (D) position. In the P/S position, splitting, projective identification, omnipotent denial, and idealization tend to dominate. Love and hate become bifurcated, and splitting results in projecting the "good" and "bad" elements into idealized and persecutory objects, respectively. Terrifying anxieties over fantasied annihilation by persecutory internal (albeit projected) objects are personified by the term *paranoid*, whereas the term *schizoid* reflects the splitting undergone in fantasy that is required to maintain a suitable relationship to the object's goodness in the face of the subject's omnipotence.

Perversion is characterized by wishful defenses that facilitate disavowal of reality in order to provide relief from terrifying anxieties. Perversion was considered by psychoanalyst Jacques Lacan to be a third structure between that of a neurotic person and a psychotic one. Though originally used exclusively in relation to psychosexuality, it is used today in relation to a plurality of instincts and defenses—including those of a more psychotic nature, such as splitting, disavowal, and archaic bodily fantasies—and it is common to speak of perverse tendencies in relation to morality, malevolence, and cruelty, as well as various psychological disturbances (such as eating disorders).

Plutocracy or ***plutarchy*** is a society ruled or controlled by people of great wealth or income. The first known use of the term in English dates from 1631. Unlike systems such as democracy, liberalism, socialism, communism, and anarchism, plutocracy is not rooted in an established political philosophy.

Populism refers to a range of political stances that emphasize—or claim to champion—an ethic of *the people* (or *the common man*) and often juxtapose this group against *the elite* (or perceived elite persons who represent the established order). In short, it is a political approach that strives to appeal to ordinary people who feel that their concerns are disregarded by established elite groups. Populist parties and social movements exist along both the left and right wings of the political spectrum and are often led by charismatic or dominant figures who present themselves as the voice of the people.

Projective identification is a term used in psychoanalysis and other professional mental health fields to refer to a fantasized object relationship that begins in the *paranoid-schizoid position* (P/S). In this position, largely intolerable, mostly "bad" parts of the self (or selves in group psychology) are split off, and in an expulsive process, they are projected into an external object (or objects), which then becomes "identified" with the split-off part as well as possessed and controlled by it. While in a mild form it is a normal occurrence in everyday life, functioning adaptively as a sort of discharge and/or as a communicative operation, it is also regarded by dint of the external object's *introjective identification* as the prototype of aggressively divisive object relations.

Psychotic refers to the most primitive part of the psyche and a form of mental functioning in which there is a withdrawal from a part of reality, so that primary processes become dominant. While the psychotic and non-psychotic parts of the personality often exist together, the psychotic aspect is intensely frustrated and often threatened by reality, and consequently, it fantasizes its destruction and its distorted restitution. In short, the awareness of reality is hated, as are elements that are reminders of it; a universe of bizarre objects is constructed that, in the Bionian sense, forecloses the ability to think.

Regression refers to going back to a more developmentally immature level of psychic functioning, particularly when there is a substantial disruption in phase-appropriate mental organization. Reflecting a return to an earlier level of functioning or mode of expression at a less sophisticated level of complexity, structure, and differentiation, regression often occurs in response to events that are experienced as psychologically traumatic. *Large-group regression* tends to be characterized by a more narcissistic, solipsistic, and part-object world in which unconscious, primary-process functioning operates in accordance with the pleasure (versus reality) principle in an effort to fulfill a more utopian, tension-free group fantasy. In Bionian terminology, group regression means that basic-assumption functioning surmounts work group, task-oriented secondary processing.

Representative democracy, also known as *indirect democracy* or *representative government*, is a type of democracy founded on the principle of elected officials representing a group of people, as opposed to direct democracy. While typically categorized as a democracy, the United States is more accurately defined as a *constitutional federal republic*. As noted earlier, the American people elect representatives to deliberate and decide on legislation, and successful governmental functioning requires a loyal opposition to the government in power without denying its legitimacy (in short, *not* an opposition to the democratic political system itself). Voters are free to choose their own preferred representatives, and when an individual's preferred candidate does not win an election, the majority's choice of a different candidate must be respected.

Republic is a form of government in which power is held by the people and their elected representatives. In republics, the country is considered a "public" matter, not the private concern or property of its rulers.

In contrast to democracy, which is an ideology that helps shape how a government is run, a republic is the system of government that allows a country to be democratic.

Second skin is a term used by psychoanalysts Vamık Volkan and Otto Kernberg to describe their conceptual broadening of the self-protective *skin-ego* of an individual psyche (an earlier psychoanalytic concept) to the large-group context. In large, regressed groups, it refers to a social structure that is sought by members in order to recover a lost sense of security that previously provided existential protection, especially an individualized identity (i.e., one largely constructed in terms of status and role relationships). Because the protective "skin" (i.e., "skin-ego" or "first skin") of normal social structures is weakened and lost under crises-based, traumatic conditions, regressed large groups seek leadership that can provide the desperately needed *second skin* through assuring that the existential security of its members will be restored.

Signal anxiety refers to the vague feeling of anxiety or dread experienced in anticipation of intrapsychic danger, especially overstimulating existential threat. Operating as a *signal*, it serves as a trigger for setting in motion defensive operations against inflowing excitations that might traumatically overwhelm the psyche. In situations of objective danger, this form of apprehensiveness is part of an adaptive response; however, in situations of excessive fears—less realistic ones—often agitated by demagogues, it can maladaptively prompt a warding off from consciousness of emerging impulses and painful feelings that can be useful for effective action.

Skin-ego indicates an essential protective shield within an individual psyche that is the foundation of the *container/contained* relationship; it interfaces between inside and outside to enable picturing the psyche itself as a vessel of mental contents. It remains a crucial aspect of the psyche in that it functions as a shielding barrier that enables mental organization to proceed by containing, registering, and managing intersensorial correspondences; consequently, it embodies a permeable contact barrier open to change.

Splitting is a primitive mental mechanism that originates in an infant's mind, in which *pleasurable/unpleasurable* as well as *good/bad* experiences are separated. This splitting mechanism thereby serves to regulate and order experience out of primal instinctual chaos. Later, this separation mechanism can serve a defensive purpose against intense ambivalence, and its extensive use is an indicator of severe character pathology.

Symbolic function (also termed *paternal function* or *triadic function*) describes the role of a "third" object or element that permits entry into the symbolic universe by separating two objects that are otherwise closely fused together. The concept originated in Freudian psychoanalysis and was later elaborated by French psychoanalysts; it initially referred to the father's symbolic task of separating the child from the mother. Because the core structure of human relatedness is triangular, *thirdness* is always necessary to promote differentiation from the perils arising from the collusive power of two closely merged or identified objects. In large groups, *the third*, by upholding the symbolic function, serves to attenuate the close merger that often entails psychotic processes occurring between the group and its leader.

Technocracy is a system of government in which a decision maker or makers are appointed or self-appointed on the basis of expertise in a given area of responsibility, particularly with regard to scientific or technical knowledge.

Totalitarianism is a form of government or political system that prohibits opposition parties, restricts individual opposition to the state and its claims, and exercises an extremely high degree of control over public and private life.

Trance logic is a common occurrence in altered mental states such as hypnosis, one in which a person's normal capacity for critical analysis is suspended, and logical inconsistencies are more easily tolerated. As a result, the individual or group in a trance state is more open to suggestion.

Tyranny is a cruel, harsh, and unfair government in which a person or small group of people have power over everyone else. Self-expression and individuality are severely limited, often by undue severity or harshness.

Work group is psychoanalyst Bion's term that refers to task-oriented groups focused on the need for change through utilizing secondary processes of rational thought, reality testing, and realistic organizational approaches to the specific group task. When functioning in this way, the group defines its task, acknowledges its purpose, and promotes cooperation among its members.

References

Acemoglu, D., & Robinson, J. A. (2020). *The Narrow Corridor: States, Societies, and the Fate of Liberty*. New York: Penguin.

Adorno, T. W. (1951). The Freudian theory and the patterns of fascist propaganda. In: A. Arato & E. Gebhardt (Eds.), *The Essential Frankfurt School Reader* (pp. 118–137). New York: Continuum, 1982.

Adorno, T. W. (1967). *Aspects of the New Right-Wing Extremism*. W. Hoban (Trans.). Cambridge: Polity, 2020.

Adorno, T. W., Frenkel-Brunswik, E., Levinson, D. J., & Sanford, R. N. (1950). *The Authoritarian Personality*. New York: Harper & Row.

Applebaum, A. (2020). *Twilight of Democracy: The Seductive Lure of Authoritarianism*. New York: Doubleday.

Arato, A., & Gebhardt, E. (Eds.) (1982). *The Essential Frankfurt School Reader*. New York: Continuum.

Arendt, H. (1951). *The Origins of Totalitarianism*. New York: Schocken.

Arendt, H. (1963). *Eichmann in Jerusalem: A Report on the Banality of Evil*. New York: Viking.

Bergstein, A. (2020). Violent emotions and the violence of life. *International Journal of Psychoanalysis, 101*: 863–878.

Bion, W. R. (1957). Differentiation of the psychotic from the non-psychotic personalities. *International Journal of Psychoanalysis, 38*: 266–275.

Bion, W. R. (1961). *Experiences in Groups and Other Papers*. London: Tavistock.

Bion, W. R. (1962). *Learning from Experience*. London: Heinemann.

Bion, W. R. (1970). *Attention and Interpretation*. New York: Basic Books.

Bleger, J. (1967). Psycho-analysis of the psycho-analytic frame. *International Journal of Psychoanalysis*, *48*: 511–519.

Bollas, C. (2018). *Meaning and Melancholia: Life in the Age of Bewilderment*. London: Routledge.

Bollas, C. (2020). Civilization and the discontented. Paper presented at Community West, Los Angeles, CA, April.

Bowes, S. M., Costello, T. H., Ma, W., & Lilienfeld, S. O. (2021). Looking under the tinfoil hat: clarifying the personological and psychopathological correlates of conspiracy beliefs. *Journal of Personality*, *89*: 422–436.

Chasseguet-Smirgel, J. (1984). *Creativity and Perversion*. New York: W. W. Norton.

Chenoweth, E., & Stephan, M. J. (2013). *Why Civil Resistance Works: The Strategic Logic of Nonviolent Conflict*. New York: Columbia University Press.

Chrzanowski, C. S. (2019). The group's vulnerability to disaster: basic assumption and work group mentalities underlying Trump's 2016 election. *International Journal of Psychoanalysis*, *100*: 711–731.

Danner, M. (2021, February 11). Be ready to fight. *New York Review of Books*, *68*: 4–8.

Diamond, M. J. (2021). *Masculinity and Its Discontents: The Male Psyche and the Inherent Tensions of Maturing Manhood*. London: Routledge.

Diamond, M. J., & Lobitz, W. C. (1973). When familiarity breeds respect: the effects of an experimental depolarization program on police and student attitudes toward each other. *Journal of Social Issues*, *29*: 95–109.

Douglas, K. M., Uscinski, J. D., Sutton, R. M., Cichocka, A., Nefes, T., Ang, C. S., & Deravi, F. (2019). Understanding conspiracy theories. *Advances in Political Psychology*, *40* (suppl. 1): 3–35.

Eco, U. (1995, June 22). Ur-fascism (eternal fascism). *New York Review of Books*, *42*(11).

Festinger, L. (1957). *A Theory of Cognitive Dissonance*. Stanford, CA: Stanford University Press.

Festinger, L., Riecken, H. W., & Schachter, S. (1956). *When Prophecy Fails: A Social and Psychological Study of a Modern Group that Predicted the Destruction of the World*. Minneapolis, MN: University of Minnesota Press/Stanford, CA: Stanford University Press.

Fishkin, J. (2018). *Democracy When People Are Thinking*. Oxford: Oxford University Press.

Fishkin, J., Siu, A., Diamond, L., & Bradburn, N. (2020). Is deliberation an antidote to extreme partisan polarization? Reflections on "America in One Room." Paper presented at 116th Annual Meeting of the American Political Science Association, San Francisco, CA, September 10–13.

Freud, S. (1921). *Group Psychology and the Analysis of the Ego. S. E., 18*: 63–143. London: Hogarth.

Freud, S. (1924a). Neurosis and psychosis. *S. E., 19*: 149–153. London: Hogarth.

Freud, S. (1924b). The loss of reality in neurosis and psychosis. *S. E., 19*: 183–187. London: Hogarth.

Freud, S. (1933). *Why War? S. E., 22*: 195–215. London: Hogarth.

Fromm, E. (1955). *The Sane Society*. New York: Rinehart.

Fromm, E. (1964). *The Heart of Man: Its Genius for Good and Evil*. New York: Harper & Row.

González, F. J. (2020). Looking beyond: toward a psychoanalytic future. *Journal of the American Psychoanalytic Association, 68*: 1101–1111.

Greenberg, A. S. (2005). *Manifest Manhood and the Antebellum American Empire*. Cambridge: Cambridge University Press.

Greenhouse, L. (2021, July 1). Grievance conservatives are here to stay. *New York Review of Books, 68*: 34–35.

Hamilton, A., Madison, J., & Jay, J. (2003). Introduction. In: R. Clinton & C. R. Kessler (Eds.), *The Federalist Papers* (Signet Classics) (pp. 1787–1788). New York: New American Library.

Hoffman, L. (2018). Psychoanalytic perspectives on populism. *Contemporary Psychoanalysis, 54*: 266–289.

Hoffman, L. (2021). The evolution of racism in the Western world: addressing fear of the other. *Journal of the American Psychoanalytic Association, 69*: 389–405.

Hofstadter, R. (1965). *The Paranoid Style in American Politics and Other Essays*. New York: Alfred A. Knopf.

Jaques, E. (1955). Social systems as a defence against persecutory and depressive anxiety: a contribution to the psycho-analytic study of social process. In: E. Jaques, M. Klein, P. Heinemann, & R. Money-Kyrle (Eds.), *New Directions in Psycho-Analysis* (pp. 478–498). London: Tavistock.

Kant, I. (1793). On the common saying: "This may be true in theory, but it does not apply in practice." In: H. Reiss (Ed.), H. B. Nisbet (Trans.), *Kant's Political Writings* (pp. 61–92). Cambridge: Cambridge University Press, 1970.

Keats, J. (1817). From a letter to George and Thomas Keats, December 21, 1817. In: J. P. Hunter (Ed.), *The Norton Introduction to Literature: The Poetry* (pp. 477–478). New York: W. W. Norton, 1973.

Kernberg, O. F. (1992). *Aggression in Personality Disorders and Perversions*. New Haven, CT: Yale University Press.

Kernberg, O. F. (2020). Malignant narcissism and large group regression. *Psychoanalytic Quarterly, 89*: 1–24.

King, V., & Schmid Noerr, G. (2020). Conceptions of the superego in sociological and socio-psychological analyses. *International Journal of Psychoanalysis, 101*: 740–756.

Klein, M. (1946). Notes on some schizoid mechanisms. In: *The Writings of Melanie Klein, Volume III: Envy and Gratitude and Other Works, 1946–1963* (pp. 1–24). New York: Free Press, 1984.

Layton, L. (2020). *Toward A Social Psychoanalysis: Culture, Character, and Normative Unconscious Processes*. New York: Routledge.

Lee, B. X. (2020). *Profile of a Nation: Trump's Mind, America's Soul*. New York: World Mental Health Coalition.

Levitsky, S., & Ziblatt, D. (2018). *How Democracies Die*. New York: Broadway.

Lifton, R. J. (2020). Owning reality: reflections on cultism and zealotry. *Journal of the American Psychoanalytic Association, 68*: 413–432.

Loewenstein, E. A. (2017). Dystopian narratives: encounters with the perverse sadomasochistic universe. *Psychoanalytic Inquiry, 37*: 3–15.

Loewenstein, E. A. (2018). The agitator and his propaganda machine: Donald Trump and the road to American fascism. *Fort Da, 24*: 40–55.

Loewenstein, E. A. (2020, August 22). In dark times: psychoanalytic praxis as a form of resistance to fascist propaganda. Paper presented at opening event, South Bay for Psychoanalytic Study, Psychoanalytic Institute of Northern California.

Löwenthal, L., & Guterman, N. (1949). *Prophets of Deceit: A Study of the Techniques of the American Agitator*. London: Verso (New Left), 2021.

MacLean, N. (2017). *Democracy in Chains: The Deep History of the Radical Right's Stealth Plan for America*. New York: Penguin.

Meltzer, D. (1992). *The Claustrum: An Investigation of Claustrophobic Phenomena*. Clunie, UK: The Roland Harris Educational Trust.

Morgan, D. (Ed.) (2019). *The Unconscious in Social and Political Life*. London: Phoenix.

Morgan, D. (Ed.) (2021). *A Deeper Cut: Further Explorations of the Unconscious in Social and Political Life*. London: Phoenix.

Moss, D. (2021). On having whiteness. *Journal of the American Psychoanalytic Association, 69*: 355–371.

Müller, J.-W. (2021). *Democracy Rules*. New York: Farrar, Straus and Giroux.

Mutz, D. C. (2018). Status threat, not economic hardship, explains 2016 presidential vote. *Proceedings of the National Academy of Sciences, 115*: 4330–4339.

Nussbaum, M. C. (2018). *The Monarchy of Fear: A Philosopher Looks at Our Political Crisis*. New York: Simon & Schuster.

Orne, M. T. (1959). The nature of hypnosis: artifact and essence. *Journal of Abnormal & Social Psychology, 58*: 277–299.

O'Toole, F. (2021, March 25). To hell with unity. *New York Review of Books, 68*: 9–11.

Packer, G. (2021a, Jan/Feb). Dispatches: the legacy of Donald Trump. *The Atlantic, 327*: 9–12.

Packer, G. (2021b). *Last Best Hope: America in Crisis and Renewal*. New York: Farrar, Straus and Giroux.

Pape, R. A., & Ruby, K. (unpublished). The face of American insurrection: right-wing organizations evolving into a violent mass movement. Report from Chicago Projects on Security & Threats (CPST), University of Chicago, Division of Social Sciences, April 2021.

Pettigrew, T. F. (2017). Social psychological perspectives on Trump supporters. *Journal of Social & Political Psychology, 5*: 107–116.

Przeworski, A. (1991). *Democracy and the Market*. New York: Cambridge University Press.

Rangell, L. (1980). *The Mind of Watergate: An Explanation of the Compromise of Integrity*. New York: W. W. Norton.

Rao, D. G. (2021). Review of Isabel Wilkerson's *Caste: The Origins of Our Discomfort*. *Journal of the American Psychoanalytic Association, 69*: 412–421.

Rhodes, B. (2021). *After the Fall: Being American in the World We've Made*. New York: Random House.

Roethke, T. (1964). In a dark time. In: *The Collected Poems of Theodore Roethke*. New York: Anchor, 1975.

Rosenfeld, H. A. (1984). Narcissism and aggression: clinical and theoretical considerations. In: H. Schoenhals Hart (Trans.), *Narcissism and Aggression Working Conference of the DPV 1984 in Wiesbaden* (pp. 65–81). Wiesbaden, Germany: DPV Conference Publication, 1985.

Rosenfeld, H. A. (1987). *Impasse and Interpretation: Therapeutic and Anti-Therapeutic Factors in the Psychoanalytical Treatment of Psychotic, Borderline, and Neurotic Patients*. London: Tavistock.

Rosenfeld, S. (2019). *Democracy and Truth: A Short History*. Philadelphia, PA: University of Pennsylvania Press.

Schedler, A. (2013). *The Politics of Uncertainty: Sustaining and Subverting Electoral Authoritarianism*. New York: Oxford University Press.

Shapiro, J. (2020). *Shakespeare in a Divided America: What His Plays Tell Us about Our Past and Future*. New York: Penguin.

Sides, J., Tesler, M., & Vavreck, L. (2019). *Identity Crisis: The 2016 Presidential Campaign and the Battle for the Meaning of America*. Princeton, NJ: Princeton University Press.

Skale, E. (2021). The rise of the new right: psychoanalytic perspectives. In: D. Morgan (Ed.), *A Deeper Cut: Further Explorations of the Unconscious in Social and Political Life* (pp. 233–245). London: Phoenix.

Snyder, T. (2017). *On Tyranny: Twenty Lessons from the Twentieth Century*. New York: Crown.

Snyder, T. (2021, January 9). The American Abyss. *New York Times Magazine*.

Steiner, J. (2020). *Illusion, Disillusion, and Irony in Psychoanalysis*. London: Routledge.

Stenner, K. (2005). *The Authoritarian Dynamic*. Cambridge: Cambridge University Press.

Stenner, K., & Haidt, J. (2018). Authoritarianism is not a momentary madness, but an eternal dynamic within liberal democracies. In: C. R. Sunstein (Ed.), *Can It Happen Here? Authoritarianism in America* (pp. 175–219). New York: HarperCollins.

Stills, S. (1966). For what it's worth (stop, hey, what's that sound). Song performed by Buffalo Springfield, released on Atco Records. Lyrics © Warner Chappell Music, Los Angeles, CA.

Stokoe, P. (2019). Where have all the adults gone? In: D. Morgan (Ed.), *The Unconscious in Social and Political Life* (pp. 1–26). London: Phoenix.

Turquet, P. (1975). Threats to identity in the large group. In: L. Kreeger (Ed.), *The Large Group: Dynamics and Therapy* (pp. 57–86). London: Constable.

Volkan, V. D. (2004). *Blind Trust: Large Groups and Their Leaders in Times of Crisis and Terror*. Charlottesville, VA: Pitchstone.

Volkan, V. D. (2020). *Large Group Psychology: Racism, Societal Divisions, Narcissistic Leaders, and Who We Are Now*. London: Phoenix.

Wilkerson, I. (2020). *Caste: The Origins of Our Discontents*. New York: Penguin Random House.

Wolf, E. S. (1988). *Treating the Self: Elements of Clinical Self Psychology*. New York: Guilford.

Woodward, B., & Costa, R. (2021). *Peril*. New York: Simon & Schuster.

Zelizer, J. D. (2020). *Burning Down the House: Newt Gingrich, the Fall of a Speaker, and the Rise of the New Republican Party*. New York: Penguin.

Ziblatt, D. (2017). *Conservative Parties and the Birth of Democracy*. Cambridge: Cambridge University Press.

Zienert-Eilts, K. J. (2020). Destructive populism as "perverted containing": a psychoanalytical look at the attraction of Donald Trump. *International Journal of Psychoanalysis, 101*: 971–991.

Index

Note: **Bold** indicates glossary references; *fn* indicates footnote.

9781800131279